Project Management:
Practice Questions for CAPM & PMP Certification Exams

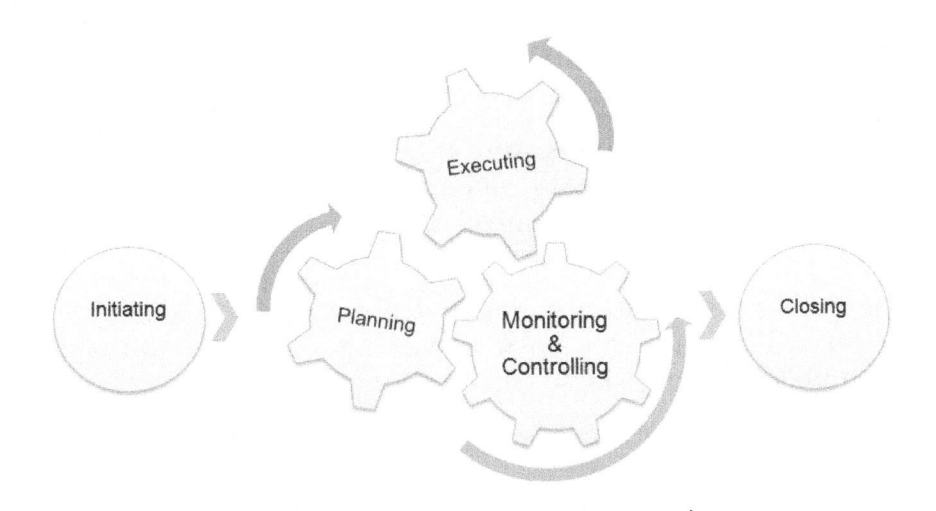

Peter Landini

- ✓ Aligned with PMBOK 6th Edition, and
- ✓ September 2019 CAPM & July 2020 PMP Exam Changes
- ✓ Separate practice tests to prepare for CAPM & PMP
- ✓ Free links to online versions of all practice tests

Project Management:
Practice Questions for CAPM
& PMP Certification Exams

Published by CreateSpace, an Amazon.com Company

Available from Amazon.com and other retail outlets

Copyright © 2019 Peter Landini

All rights reserved.

PMI, PMBOK, CAPM, and PMP are registered marks of the Project Management Institute, Inc.

The contents of this book were produced independently and have not been authorized, sponsored, or approved by the Project Management Institute (PMI)

The author issues no warrant that the use of this book and associated media will ensure passing of any exams, or qualifying for professional certification.

Thank you for buying an authorized edition of this book and for complying with copyright laws by not reproducing, scanning, or distributing any part of it in any form or media without permission.

ISBN: 9781692528454

CONTENTS

About the Book	1
2019 Exam Content Changes	2
About the Author	3
Project Management Checklist	4

PRACTICE QUESTIONS

- Set #1: 50 CAPM/knowledge questions — 9
- Set #2: 50 CAPM/knowledge questions — 23
- Set #3: 50 CAPM/knowledge questions — 37
- Set #4: 50 CAPM/knowledge questions — 51
- Set #5: 50 PMP/situational questions — 63
- Set #6: 50 PMP/situational questions — 79
- Set #7: 50 PMP/leadership questions — 97
- Set #8: 50 PMP/agile questions — 111

ONLINE

- Links to interactive versions, including CAPM 150-Question Practice Test, and PMP 200-Question Practice Test, and Additional Study Tools — 125

ANSWERS — 127

ABOUT THE BOOK

The purpose of this book is to provide assessment and self-evaluation tools to students preparing for CAPM (Certified Associate in Project Management) or PMP (Project Management Professional) certification exams.

The **Project Management Checklist** is a brief section of key concepts and terminology that one should understand prior to working with the practice questions.

Following section of **Practice Questions** will present 400 multiple choice questions that cover the full breadth of project management as defined by the *Guide to the Project Management Body of Knowledge – 6th Edition.* **(Project Management Institute; 2017)** aka, *PMBOK*.

The first four sets of 50 questions are considered knowledge based questions, for both CAPM & PMP candidates to evaluate their understanding of the core material. Question Sets #5 through #8 are meant for PMP candidates, as they require analysis of a given situation and may refer to specific leadership skills, PMI's *Agile Practice Guide* and *Code of Ethics and Professional Responsibility*.

It is highly recommended that all readers of this book obtain the PMBOK Guide, and that PMP candidates also obtain the Agile Practice Guide. For more information on PMI and their professional certification prerequisites, education & experience requirement, and exam outlines visit their website at www.pmi.org

The **ONLINE** section of this publication contains links to the interactive versions of all practice tests found in the book. These will provide you with a score immediately upon completion, along with an indication of which questions you answered correctly, or incorrectly, and an explanation containing reference to the PMBOK Guide.

The last section **STUDY TOOLS** are described in this text and available through the online links. These tools focus on learning and understanding the 5 Project Management Processes, 10 Knowledge Areas, 49 Project Management Processes, and their Inputs, Tools & Techniques, and Outputs. There are also additional exercises to challenge one's skills in project scheduling and cost controls.

2019/20 EXAM CONTENT CHANGES

CAPM Exam Changes:

PMI has announced changes to the CAPM exam to take effect September 1, 2019. While the exam will remain based on the PMBOK 6th Edition, two new question formats will be introduced in addition to standard multiple choice questions :

(1) **Matching**: These questions require you to match choices from the right column to terms given in the left column. You will not receive partial credit for an incomplete or partially correct response.

(2) **Multiple Selection:** These questions require you to select two or more correct answers from the multiple choice selections to get credit. You will not receive partial credit for an incomplete or partially correct response.

These question formats are included in CAPM Question Sets #1-4, and in the online CAPM 150-Question Practice Test.

PMP Exam Changes:

PMI has announced changes to the PMP exam to take effect July 1, 2020. While the exam will continue to refer to PMBOK 6th Edition, it will be recalibrated to increase the emphasis placed on :

(1) **Leadership, Communications, and other 'Soft Skills',**

(2) **Agile/Adaptive project life cycles.**

The revised exam structure will focus on People, Process, and Business Environment as domains to align the PMP exam with the core project manager competencies defined in the *Talent Triangle*.

In addition to the *PMBOK Guide* and the *Code of Ethics and Professional Conduct*, questions will also refer to material in PMI's *Agile Practice Guide*.

To address these changes and support students through PMI's transition to the new PMP exam, PMP Question Sets #5-6 will continue to focus on PMBOK Methodology & Process related questions appropriate for pre-July 1, 2020 exams, while PMP Question Set #7 will focus on Leadership skills, and Question Set #8 will focus on the Agile/Adaptive approaches introduced in exams after July 1, 2020. Online PMP 200-Question Practice Tests will be available in both formats through this transition.

ABOUT THE AUTHOR

Peter Landini worked in various capacities of project and program management since 1979. Primarily involved with technology integration projects, Pete managed projects in retail, financial services, entertainment and telecommunications industries. He earned his Bachelor of Science degree in Management & Communications from Adelphi University, and a Masters Certificate in Project Management from The George Washington University, as well as certifying as PMP (*Project Management Professional*), SSLBB (*Six Sigma Lean Black Belt Professional*), and PSM (*Professional Scrum Master*).

Peter currently teaches Project Management and related courses at Nassau Community College, Suffolk County Community College, and Long Island University.

PROJECT MANAGEMENT CHECKLIST

The Project Management Context
- ✓ Project vs. Operations
- ✓ Projects, Programs, and Portfolios
- ✓ The Project Life Cycle
- ✓ Predictive/Waterfall vs. Adaptive/Agile
- ✓ Phases, Deliverables, Milestones, Phase-Gates
- ✓ Work Performance Data, Information, and Reports
- ✓ Five (5) Project Management Process Groups
- ✓ Ten (10) Project Management Knowledge Areas

The Project Environment
- ✓ Enterprise Environmental Factors
- ✓ Operational Process Assets
- ✓ Governance Frameworks
- ✓ Organizational Structure Types
- ✓ The Project Management Office (PMO)
- ✓ The Project Sponsor

The Project Manager's Roles & Responsibilities
- ✓ Project Manager's Sphere of Influence
- ✓ Project Manager Competences
- ✓ The PMI Talent Triangle
- ✓ Technical Project Management
- ✓ Strategic and Business Management
- ✓ Leadership Styles
- ✓ Situational Leadership
- ✓ The Servant Leader
- ✓ Source of Power/Authority

Project Integration Management
- ✓ Business Case
- ✓ Project Benefits Management Plan
- ✓ Project Charter
- ✓ Objectives, Contraints, Boundaries, Assumptions
- ✓ Kick-off Meeting
- ✓ The Project Management Plan
- ✓ Project Baselines
- ✓ Integrated Change Control
- ✓ Project Closing

Project Scope Management
- ✓ Project Scope vs. Product Scope
- ✓ Requirements Document & Traceability Matrix
- ✓ Scope Statement
- ✓ Acceptance Criteria
- ✓ Progressive Elaboration
- ✓ Scope Creep
- ✓ Work Breakdown Structure (WBS)
- ✓ Verified Deliverables vs Accepted Deliverables

Project Schedule Management
- ✓ Activity & Milestone Lists
- ✓ Precedence Diagramming Method (PDM)
- ✓ Dependencies: Predecessors & Successors
- ✓ Dependencies: Mandatory vs Discretionary
- ✓ Dependencies: Internal vs External
- ✓ Leads and Lags
- ✓ Time Estimates: Analogous, Parametric, 3-Point
- ✓ Critical Path Method (CPM)
- ✓ Total Float
- ✓ Resource Optimization (Resource Leveling)
- ✓ Schedule Compression: Crashing & Fast-Tracking
- ✓ Gantt Chart

Project Cost Management
- ✓ Cost Estimates: Analogous, Parametric, 3-Point
- ✓ Funding Limit Reconciliation
- ✓ Earned Value Management
- ✓ Planned Value (PV)
- ✓ Earned Value (EV)
- ✓ Actual Cost (AC)
- ✓ Schedule Variance (SV = EV-PV)
- ✓ Cost Variance (CV = EV-AC)
- ✓ Schedule Performance Index (SPI = EV/PV)
- ✓ Cost Performance Index (CPI = EV/AC)
- ✓ Budget at Completion (BAC)
- ✓ Estimate at Completion (EAC)
- ✓ Estimate to Complete (ETC)
- ✓ Forecasting Atypical Variance: ETC = BAC-EV
- ✓ Forecasting Typical Variances: ETC = (BAC-EV)/CPI
- ✓ Forecasting: EAC = AC+ETC
- ✓ To-Complete Performance Index (BAC-EV)/(BAC-AC)

Project Quality Management
- ✓ Cost of Quality
- ✓ Cost of Conformance: Prevention & Appraisal Costs
- ✓ Cost of Non-Conformance: Internal & External
- ✓ Quality vs. Grade
- ✓ Manage Quality vs. Control Quality
- ✓ Process Improvement Plan
- ✓ Quality Tools: Fishbone Diagram (Ishikawa)
- ✓ Quality Tools: Flowcharts
- ✓ Quality Tools: Checklists
- ✓ Quality Tools: Pareto Diagram
- ✓ Quality Tools: Histogram
- ✓ Quality Tools: Control Chart
- ✓ Quality Tools: Scatter Diagram
- ✓ Attributes Sampling vs. Variables Sampling

Project Resource Management
- ✓ Project Roles & Responsibilities
- ✓ RACI: Responsible, Accountable, Consult, Inform
- ✓ Resource Estimates: Analogous, Parametric, 3-Point
- ✓ Resource Breakdown Structure
- ✓ Personnel, Materials, and Equipment
- ✓ Project Team Assignments
- ✓ Physical Resource Assignments
- ✓ Virtual vs. Co-located teams
- ✓ Tuckman's Ladder: Stages of Team Development
- ✓ Conflict Resolution

Project Communications Management
- ✓ Communications Management Plan
- ✓ Communications Channels = $n(n-1)/2$
- ✓ Methods, Media, and Technology
- ✓ The Communication Model
- ✓ Communication Skills
- ✓ The Five C's of Communication
- ✓ Transparency
- ✓ Active Listening
- ✓ Facilitating a Meeting

Project Risk Management
- ✓ Risk Appetite
- ✓ Threats vs. Opportunities
- ✓ The Risk Register
- ✓ Qualitative Risk Analysis
- ✓ Probability, Impact, and Urgency
- ✓ Quantitative Risk Analysis
- ✓ Monte Carlo Simulation and Tornado Diagram
- ✓ Decision Tree Analysis
- ✓ Contingency Reserve vs. Management Reserve
- ✓ Risk Responses: Strategies for Threats
- ✓ Risk Responses: Strategies for Opportunities

Project Procurement Management
- ✓ Make or Buy Analysis
- ✓ Source Selection Criteria
- ✓ Statement of Work
- ✓ Request for Proposal vs. Request for Quotation
- ✓ Fixed Price vs. Cost Reimbursable Contracts
- ✓ Incentive-based Contracts
- ✓ Time & Materials Contracts
- ✓ Control Procurements

Project Stakeholder Management
- ✓ Stakeholder Register
- ✓ Stakeholder Engagement Matrix (Current/Desired)
- ✓ Salience Model (Power, Influence, Legitimacy)
- ✓ Interpersonal and Team Skills

Considerations for Agile/Adaptive Environments
- ✓ Suitability factors
- ✓ Hybrid project life cycles
- ✓ Scrum, Kanban, Agile Unified Process, LeSS, SAFe
- ✓ Planning for Iteration & Flow-based approaches
- ✓ Product Backlog preparation & refinement
- ✓ Increments and the Minimum Viable Product
- ✓ Standup Meetings
- ✓ Metrics: Burndown, Burnup, EVM in Agile environment
- ✓ Inspection, Adaptation, and Transparency
- ✓ Demonstrations/Reviews
- ✓ Retrospectives
- ✓ Scalability

Practice Questions Set #1

50 multiple choice questions

CAPM
Knowledge Based Questions

Practice Question Set #1

1. A Project is:
○ A. A collection of sequential activities performed by an individual or a team.
○ B. A revenue-generating activity that needs to be accomplished within a specific time frame in order to maintain the organization's financial solvency.
○ C. An ongoing endeavor undertaken to meet customer or market requirements.
○ D. A temporary endeavor undertaken to create a unique product, service, or result.

2. The PMI Talent Triangle focuses on which three project manager competencies:
○ A. Scope, Schedule, and Cost
○ B. Technical Project Management, Leadership, and Strategic & Business Management
○ C. Predictive, Adaptive, and Iterative
○ D. Forming, Storming, and Norming

3. Portfolio management refers to:
○ A. Managing the various contents of a project folder
○ B. Managing the performance of two or more projects
○ C. Managing projects, programs, and other related operational work to achieve specific strategic business objectives.
○ D. Managing various projects for several client companies

4. The two major categories of influences that can have an impact on a project environment are:
○ A. Business Case and Project Benefits Management Plan
○ B. Enterprise Environmental Factors and Organizational Process Assets
○ C. Project Phases and Project Management Processes
○ D. Project Charter and Project Management Plan

5. The series of phases that a project passes through from its start to its completion is known as the:

○ A. Project waterfall.

○ B. Project life cycle.

○ C. Project life stages.

○ D. Project Management Process Groups.

6. All of the following are true about project phases and the project life cycle, EXCEPT:

○ A. Project risk and uncertainty are greatest at the start of the project and decrease over the life of the project.

○ B. The ability to influence the final characteristics of the final product is easiest at the start of the project.

○ C. The cost of changes typically will increase substantially as the project approaches completion.

○ D. Cost and staffing levels are generally steady throughout the project life cycle.

7. A project life cycle where scope, schedule, and cost for the entire project is planned during an early phase is known as:

○ A. Predictive Life Cycle

○ B. Adaptive Life Cycle

○ C. Incremental Life Cycle

○ D. Functional Life Cycle

8. The Initiating process group consists of the processes performed to:

○ A. Define a new project or a new phase of an existing project by obtaining authorization to start the project or phase.

○ B. Deploy risk mitigation strategies to enhance the likelihood of project success

○ C. Conduct an audit to ensure project compliance with organizational standards

○ D. Approve the market analysis to ensure resolution of potential contract disputes.

9. Match the Project Management Process on the left with the appropriate Process Group in the right column:

_____ Close Project or Phase   1. Initiating
_____ Develop Project Charter   2. Planning
_____ Acquire Resources   3. Executing
_____ Develop Project Schedule   4. Monitoring & Controlling
_____ Perform Integrated   5. Closing
      Change Control

10. Defining quality standards and how the project will demonstrate compliance should be performed in the:

○ A. Conceptual phase.
○ B. Planning process.
○ C. Project implementation phase.
○ D. Identify Risks process.

11. The relationship between Project Management Process Groups and project life cycle phases is best described as:

○ A. They are unrelated, incompatible concepts
○ B. They are the same concept, simply described by different terms.
○ C. Project life cycle phases interact within each Process Group, and are normally repeated within every process.
○ D. Process Groups interact within each project phase and are normally repeated for each phase.

12. Which of the following are True statements describing the Project Charter (select 3):

☐ A. It formally authorizes a project.
☐ B. It is approved by the Project Sponsor
☐ C. It defines how the project is to be executed, monitored, controlled, and closed
☐ D. It provides the project manager with the authority to apply resources to project activities
☐ E. It describes in full detail the product requirements and acceptance criteria.

13. Which process is included in the Project Integration Management knowledge area?

○ A. Develop Project Management Plan.
○ B. Control Scope
○ C. Scope Verification.
○ D. Identify Stakeholders

14. Which of the following is an acceptable cause for "re-baselining" a $10 million project?

○ A. A change to project scope with a $150,000 budget increase and a 2-week schedule extension is approved.
○ B. A supplier has instituted a new quality assurance program which has taken 18 months to implement at a cost over $1,000,000.
○ C. Productivity in the Design Dept. is lower than estimated, and as a result a 2-week delay is expected.
○ D. The Engineering Department has converted to a new $250,000 CAD system.

15. A change control board (CCB) is:

○ A. A formally constituted group of stakeholders responsible for ensuring that only a minimal amount of changes occur on the project.
○ B. A formal or an informal group of stakeholders that has oversight of project execution.
○ C. A formally constituted group of stakeholders responsible for reviewing, evaluating, approving, or rejecting changes to a project.
○ D. A report that provides project change information.

16. All of the following are true about the project scope management plan EXCEPT:

○ A. It provides guidance on how project scope will be defined, documented, managed, and controlled
○ B. It provides guidance on how project scope will be verified
○ C. It may be tailored based upon the needs of the project.
○ D. It is separate from the project management plan.

17. Collect Requirements is the process of defining and documenting stakeholder needs to meet project objective All of the following are true about this process, EXCEPT:

○ A. The project's success is directly influenced by the care taken in capturing and managing requirements.
○ B. Requirements include the documented needs and expectations of the sponsor, customer, and other stakeholders.
○ C. Requirements become the foundation of the work breakdown structure (WBS)
○ D. The development of requirements begins with an analysis of the information contained in the risk register.

18. Which of the following statements is true about the work breakdown structure (WBS)?

○ A. The WBS is a decomposition of project deliverables.
○ B. The WBS is a decomposition of project activities.
○ C. The WBS is a decomposition of project resources.
○ D. The WBS is a decomposition of project risks.

19. Which of the following is true about the Validate Scope process?

○ A. It is the process of formalizing acceptance of the completed project deliverables
○ B. Is not necessary if the project completes on time and within budget.
○ C. Occurs primarily when revisions or changes are made to project scope.
○ D. It is primarily concerned with correctness of the deliverables, while Control Quality is primarily concerned with acceptance.

20. Outputs of Define Activities includes all of the following, EXCEPT:

○ A. Activity List
○ B. Precedence Diagram
○ C. Activity Attributes
○ D. Milestone List

Project Management Practice Questions for CAPM & PMP Exams

21. In the Agile project life cycle, requirements are:
○ A. Collected in a Product Backlog, prioritized, and selected for a time-boxed Increment.
○ B. Estimated in order to determine the time frame of an Increment.
○ C. Collected, documented, and approved for the final project deliverable prior to commencing any development work.
○ D. Estimated using buffers to allow flexibility in overall project scheduling.

22. Analogous duration estimating :
○ A. Is the same as bottom-up estimating.
○ B. Uses historical information and expert judgement.
○ C. Uses a mathematical algorithm to determine durations.
○ D. Uses a weighted average of Optimistic, Pessimistic, and Most Likely estimations.

23. The critical path is established by calculating :
○ A. The activity path with the shortest duration
○ B. The activity path with the longest duration
○ C. The activity path with the greatest total float
○ D. The activity path with the most mandatory dependencies

Complete the following Critical Path Method Schedule to answer questions #24 and #25:

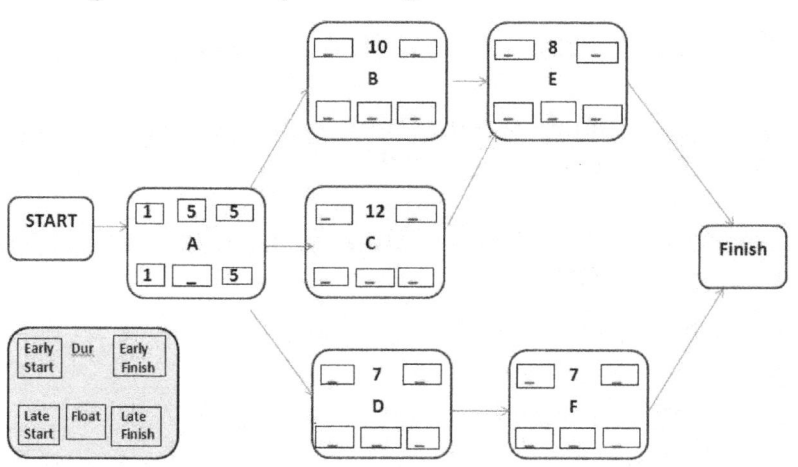

24. Which is the Critical Path:
○ A. Path A-B-E
○ B. Path A-C-E
○ C. Path A-D-F
○ D. Path A-C-F

25. Which non-critical path has the greatest total float:
○ A. Path A-B-E
○ B. Path A-C-E
○ C. Path A-D-F
○ D. Path A-C-F

26. Which of the following are methods of schedule compression (select 2):
☐ A. Float
☐ B. Lead
☐ C. Crashing
☐ D. Lag
☐ E. Fast Tracking
☐ F. Slacking

27. Crashing an activity will:
○ A. Lower overall project costs
○ B. Result in a change of project scope
○ C. Compress the schedule by adding human or physical resources to an activity.
○ D. Lengthen the schedule duration by reducing resources on an activity

28. Project Cost Management includes all of the following processes EXCEPT:
- ○ A. Estimate Costs
- ○ B. Estimate Activity Resources
- ○ C. Determine Budget
- ○ D. Control Costs

29. Three Point Estimating uses which of the following factors to calculate an estimation (select 3):
- ☐ A. Optimistic
- ☐ B. Pessimistic
- ☐ C. Analogous
- ☐ D. Most Likely
- ☐ E. Least Likely
- ☐ F. Parametric

30. In Earned Value Management, Cost Variance (CV) is equal to:
- ○ A. EV minus PV
- ○ B. EV minus AC
- ○ C. AC minus EV
- ○ D. PV minus EV

31. Consider the following cumulative measures:

　　Budget at Completion (BAC) = 200

　　Actual Costs (AC) = 120

　　Earned Value (EV) = 80

　　Cost Performance Index (CPI) = 0.666

Predicting that all future work will be accomplished at the budgeted rate, the Estimate At Completion (EAC) is:
- ○ A. 120
- ○ B. 200
- ○ C. 240
- ○ D. 300

Use the following Earned Value Management parameters to answer Questions #32 and #33:

Item	PV	AC	EV
1	10,000	11,000	10,000
2	9,000	8,000	7,000
3	8,000	8,000	8,000
4	7,000	7,000	5,000

32. Which item is MOST over budget?
- A. Item 1
- B. Item 2
- C. Item 3
- D. Item 4

33. Which item has the LOWEST Schedule Performance Index (SPI) ?
- A. Item 1
- B. Item 2
- C. Item 3
- D. Item 4

34. One of the fundamental tenets of modern quality management states that:
- A. Quality is planned and inspected in.
- B. Quality does not have costs.
- C. Quality is planned, designed, and built in—not inspected in.
- D. Quality costs are funded through management reserves.

35. Money spent during the project to avoid failures is known as the Cost of Conformance. Select the terms below that would be considered among these costs (select 4):

☐ A. Training
☐ B. Equipment
☐ C. Time To Do It Right
☐ D. Inspections
☐ E. Rework
☐ F. Scrap
☐ G. Warranty Work

36. The Quality Management process used to identify ineffective processes and causes of poor quality is known as:

○ A. Control Quality
○ B. Manage Quality
○ C. Attribute Sampling
○ D. Variables Sampling

37. A process is Out of Control when ____ data points exceed Control Limits, or ____ consecutive points are above or below the mean.

○ A. 1 / 7
○ B. 1 / 3
○ C. 3 / 7
○ D. 7 / 3

38. Plan Resource Management includes:

○ A. Developing a competitive employee compensation plan
○ B. Defining management succession and business continuity plans
○ C. Defining the staffing polices and onboarding procedures for the organization
○ D. Defining how project resources will be acquired and utilized throughout the project life cycle

Project Management Practice Questions for CAPM & PMP Exams

39. Generally acknowledged techniques for resolving conflict include (select 5):
- ☐ A, Avoid
- ☐ B. Collocate
- ☐ C. Accommodate
- ☐ D. Force
- ☐ E. Compromise
- ☐ F. Conspire
- ☐ G. Collaborate

40. Match the RACI term on the left with the appropriate responsibility level from the right column:

_____	Responsible	1. Those participating in doing the work to complete the task
_____	Accountable	2. The one ultimately answerable for the completion of a deliverable or task
_____	Consult	3. Those whose opinions are sought, and with whom there is two-way communication.
_____	Inform	4. Those that are kept up to date on progress, often where there is one-way communication

41. You send an email to members of the project team. This is an example of which Communication Method:
- ○ A. Interactive
- ○ B. Iterative
- ○ C. Push
- ○ D. Pull

42. As part of the communications process, the sender must:
- ○ A. Ensure the receiver agrees with the message.
- ○ B. Confirm that the information is properly understood.
- ○ C. Provide acknowledgment to the receiver.
- ○ D. Decode the medium correctly.

43. The total number of potential communication channels for a project with n=12 stakeholders is:

○ A. 66

○ B. 88

○ C. 47

○ D. 132

44. To be successful, the organization should be committed to address risk management:

○ A. Just in time before a meeting with major stakeholders of the project.

○ B. Proactively and consistently throughout the project.

○ C. As soon as time and cost estimates are ready.

○ D. As early as possible in the execution phase.

45. The main output of the Identify Risks process is:

○ A. Risk Register

○ B. Monte Carlo Simulation

○ C. Management Reserves

○ D. Risk Mitigation Plan

46. In the knowledge area Project Risk Management, we Plan Risk Responses and Implement Risk Responses for both threats and opportunities. From the list below, match the responses in the right column to the appropriate type of risk listed in the left column:

_____	Threat	1.	Accept
_____	Opportunity	2.	Enhance
_____	Both Threats & Opportunities	3.	Avoid

47. Generally, an RFQ (Request for Quotation) differs from an RFP (Request for Proposal) in that:

○ A. RFP is used when seller selection will be based on price.

○ B. RFP is used when the project time frame is limited.

○ C. RFQ is used when the seller selection decision will be based on price.

○ D. RFQ is used when a seller's technical capabilities and approach are critical decision drivers.

48. In which type of contract must the buyer precisely specify the product or services being procured?

○ A. Cost plus fee contract

○ B. Fixed-price contract

○ C. Cost-reimbursable contract

○ D. Partnership contract

49. The agreement that defines the type, quantity, and price of items the buyer has agreed to purchase is called:

○ A. Service Level Agreement

○ B. Purchase Order

○ C. Accounts Payable

○ D. SKU

50. Which of the following is always true about project stakeholders?

○ A. They are persons or organizations that are actively supportive of the project.

○ B. They are persons or organizations who are actively involved in the project.

○ C. They are persons or organizations whose interests may be positively or negatively affected by the performance or completion of the project.

○ D. They are persons or organizations who make the executive-level strategic decisions within the organization.

Practice Questions Set #2

50 multiple choice questions

CAPM
Knowledge Based Questions

Practice Question Set #2

1. The Project Manager is the person:

○ A. assigned by the organization to lead the team to achieve project objectives.

○ B. responsible for meeting the organization's strategic goals

○ C. responsible for completing the work requiring the greatest technical expertise and subject matter knowledge.

○ D. assigned by the organization to eliminate waste and maximize overall profitability.

2. Which of the following terms below are used in describing a Project Management Office (select 3) :

☐ A. Directing
☐ B. Operating
☐ C. Performing
☐ D. Controlling
☐ E. Supporting

3. A collection of projects that are managed in a coordinated way is called a:

○ A. Mega Project
○ B. Enterprise Project
○ C. Shared Initiative
○ D. Program

4. A _____ is a control point where deliverables are inspected to determine whether the project should continue onto its next phase, if changes or re-work is necessary, or if the project should be terminated.

○ A. Plan
○ B. Phase Gate
○ C. Waterfall
○ D. Stakeholder

5. The cost of change is:

○ A. Highest at project initiation and decreases over the project life cycle.

○ B. Lowest at project initiation and increases over the project life cycle.

○ C. Constant throughout the project life cycle.

○ D. High until deliverables are inspected, then decreases sharply.

6. The Process Group that provides feedback to implement corrective action is:

○ A. Initiating

○ B. Planning

○ C. Executing

○ D. Monitoring and Controlling

7. The Closing process group includes:

○ A. Decomposition of deliverables

○ B. Transition of ongoing operational responsibilities

○ C. Estimation of project costs

○ D. Approval of project changes

8. The Business Case is input to which Project Integration process:

○ A. Develop Project Management Plan

○ B. Develop Project Charter

○ C. Direct and Manage Project Work

○ D. Close Project or Phase

9. Lessons Learned from a previous project are considered:

○ A. Organizational Process Assets

○ B. Enterprise Environmental Factors

○ C. Progressive Elaboration

○ D. Agreements

10. Which process is used to implement approved change requests:
- ○ A. Develop Project Management Plan
- ○ B. Perform Integrated Change Control
- ○ C. Monitor and Control Project Work
- ○ D. Direct and Manage Project Work

11. The process Direct and Manage Project Work will produce the following as output (select 3):
- ☐ A. Deliverables
- ☐ B. Work Performance Data
- ☐ C. Work Performance Reports
- ☐ D. Change Requests
- ☐ E. Schedule Forecasts

12. The Scope Baseline refers to:
- ○ A. What is currently known and approved by project sponsor and stakeholders.
- ○ B. The working assumptions of the subject matter experts responsible for completing the work.
- ○ C. The scope as it was defined in the Project Charter.
- ○ D. The scope value as it was presented in the Business Case.

13. The process of updating the scope statement as it evolves over time is known as:
- ○ A. Tuckman's Ladder
- ○ B. Parkinson's Law
- ○ C. Progressive Elaboration
- ○ D. Enterprise Environmental Factors

14. Which of the following are among the Tools and Techniques of the process Collect Requirements (select 3):
- ☐ A. Observation/Conversation
- ☐ B. Focus Groups
- ☐ C. Inspection
- ☐ D. Interviews
- ☐ E. Decomposition

15. The lowest level of decomposition in the WBS is called:
○ A. a task
○ B. an activity
○ C. a deliverable
○ D. a work package

16. In the Precedence Diagram Method, a lag refers to:
○ A. a fixed delay imposed on a predecessor.
○ B. a conditional delay caused by uncertainty.
○ C. the amount of time a successor can be initiated in advance.
○ D. a slow moving resource

17. Match the dependency relationship type on the left with its definition in the right column:

_____	Finish-to-Start	1.	Predecessor may not finish until the Successor starts.
_____	Start-to-Start	2.	Successor may not finish until the Predecessor is complete.
_____	Finish-to-Finish	3.	Successor may not start until the Predecessor is complete.
_____	Start-to-Finish	4.	Successor may not start until the Predecessor starts.

18. A Discretionary Dependency is:
○ A. always depicted as a finish-to-start relationship
○ B. a conditional delay caused by uncertainty.
○ C. an activity relationship based on a preferred approach that is not absolutely required
○ D. a successor relationship based on a mandatory condition that must abide

19. An estimate is provided based on a set rate of 2 hours per unit. Your project requires 60 units, therefore 120 hours. This is an example of which estimation technique:
○ A. Analagous
○ B. Parametric
○ C. Three-Point - Triangular
○ D. Three-Point - Beta

20. In the contect of an Agile Life Cycle, the Product Backlog refers to:

○ A. The time it will take for all necessary resources to arrive on the job site.
○ B. The number of days the iteration needs in order to complete the work
○ C. The collection of requirements to be estimated, prioritized and selected for inclusion for an iteration.
○ D. The current market demand for your project's deliverables.

21. Which is NOT among the Tools and Techniques of the Estimate Costs process:

○ A. Alternatives Analysis
○ B. Reserve Analysis
○ C. Cost of Quality
○ D. Funding Limit Reconciliation

22. A project has a budget of $20,000. The planned value is currently $6,000. The project is 25% complete and $6,000 has been spent. Which statement is correct:

○ A. The project is behind schedule
○ B. The project is ahead of schedule
○ C. The project is on schedule
○ D. The project is under budget

23. Outputs of the Control Costs process include:

○ A. Work Performance Information, Cost Forecasts, and Change Requests
○ B. Work Performance Data, Cost Estimates, and Project Funding Requirements
○ C. Work Packages, Cost Baseline, and Reserve Analysis
○ D. Work Breakdown Structure, Cost Aggregation, and Funding Limit Reconciliation

24. Given the following factors:
   Earned Value = $14,000
   Planned Value = $15,000
   Actual Costs = $12,000

What is the Cost Variance?

○ A. $0
○ B. $1,000
○ C. $2,000
○ D. $3,000

25. Match the Project Quality Tool on the left with its purpose from the right column:

____	Fishbone Diagram	1.	Record measurements relative to Upper and Lower Control Limits
____	Flow Chart	2.	Perform Root Cause Analysis
____	Checksheets	3.	Data representation of statistical distribution
____	Pareto Chart	4.	Identify the most common causes
____	Histogram	5.	Determine the correlation of two variables
____	Control Chart	6.	Record variables and attributes during Inspection
____	Scatter Diagram	7.	Illustrate how various elements interrelate

26. Variables Sampling is used in Project Quality Management to determine conformity based on:

○ A. a continuous scale that measures the degree of conformity found in results under inspection

○ B. the presence (or absence) of a specific characteristic or attribute in each of the units under inspection

○ C. the costs associated with the grade of the product

○ D. the costs associated with project re-work due to poor quality

Project Management Practice Questions for CAPM & PMP Exams

27. The Cost of Non-Conformance includes:
○ A. Prevention and Appraisal costs.
○ B. Money spent during the project to avoid failures.
○ C. Internal and External Failure Costs.
○ D. Cost of Inspection and Destructive Testing Loss

28. The Resource Breakdown Structure will decompose the _____ required to complete the project work:
○ A. Resources, Issues, and Risks
○ B. Personnel, Material, and Equipment
○ C. Personnel, Contracts, and Agreements
○ D. Scope, Schedules, and Costs

29. In a Virtual team:
○ A. Technology is utilized to facilitate communications.
○ B. Team members engage in on-site activities.
○ C. A 'War Room' is reserved for the duration of the project to conduct project meetings.
○ D. Relocation is used to bring specialized expertise into to the project team.

30. Match the Stage of Team Development on the left with the appropriate description on the right:

_____	Forming	1.	Team members begin to trust each other, adjust their work habits and behaviors in support of the team.
_____	Storming	2.	Team completes the work and moves on from the project
_____	Norming	3.	Team meets and learns about the project and their roles and responsibilities
_____	Performing	4.	Team functions as a well-organized unit, working independently and effectively
_____	Adjourning	5.	Team begins to address project work and may disagree on the interpretation of project objectives or how best to accomplish project goals.

31. Using an online "live chat" function is an example of this communication method:
- A. Push
- B. Pull
- C. Iterative
- D. Interactive

32. You receive an email from a vendor that uses unfamiliar terms and abbreviations. This is considered:
- A. Noise
- B. Feedback
- C. Channel
- D. Acknowledgment

33. The project manager receives an estimate from a service provider, with an explanation of the assumptions. A copy is also sent to the project sponsor. The encoding was performed by:
- A. The project manager
- B. The service provider
- C. The project sponsor
- D. The project manager and sponsor

34. The receiver responds with disagreement to your message. According to the communication model, this is an example of:
- A. the receiver providing acknowledgment
- B. the sender providing a noise
- C. the receiver providing feedback
- D. the receiver providing noise

35. A risk with a potential positive outcome is called a:
- A. Threat
- B. Reserve
- C. Opportunity
- D. Contingency

Project Management Practice Questions for CAPM & PMP Exams

36. The Perform Qualitative Risk Analysis process assesses the priority of identified risks using which of the following (select 3):
- ☐ A. Data Simulations
- ☐ B. Urgency
- ☐ C. Probability
- ☐ D. Monte Carlo Method
- ☐ E. Tornado Diagram
- ☐ F. Impact

37. You are presented with the following project risks.

Risk ID	Probability	Impact
R1	40%	$1,000
R2	30%	$2,000
R3	10%	$5,000
R4	50%	$800

What is the total Expected Monetary Value calculated for contingency reserve:
- ○ A. $1,300
- ○ B. $1,900
- ○ C. $8,800
- ○ D. $9,800

38. The risk strategy that shifts the impact of a threat to a third party is called:
- ○ A. risk response
- ○ B. risk mitigation
- ○ C. risk transfer
- ○ D. risk acceptance

39. Inputs to Plan Risk Responses include:
- ○ A. Risk Mitigation and Risk Reserves
- ○ B. Risk Register and Change Requests
- ○ C. Qualitative Risk Analysis and Quantitative Risk Analysis
- ○ D. Risk Register and Risk Management Plan

40. The process of Plan Procurement Management will produce the following outputs, EXCEPT:
- ○ A. Procurement Management Plan
- ○ B. Make-or-Buy Decision
- ○ C. Agreements
- ○ D. Source Selection Criteria

41. Of the following contract types, which requires the seller to assume the risk of cost overruns?
- ○ A. Fixed Cost
- ○ B. Time and Materials
- ○ C. Cost Reimburseable
- ○ D. Cost Plus Fixed fee

42. The procurement document that requests potential sellers to provide a price to perform all the detailed work specified by the buyer is known as a:
- ○ A. Request for Quotation
- ○ B. Request for Information
- ○ C. Request for Proposal
- ○ D. Request for Submission

43. In which Project Procurement Management process does Negotiation occur:
- ○ A. Plan Procurement Management
- ○ B. Conduct Procurements
- ○ C. Control Procurements
- ○ D. Close Procurements

44. Stakeholders can be identified:
- ○ A. Only within Project Initiation
- ○ B. Within any of the five project management process groups
- ○ C. Within Project Initiation and Monitoring & Controlling process groups
- ○ D. Only within Project Planning

45. Which of the following is a Tool & Technique of Manage Stakeholder Engagement, categorized as Interpersonal and Team Skills:

- A. Mind Mapping
- B. Benchmarking
- C. Configuration Management
- D. Cultural Awareness

46. Plan Stakeholder Management is primarily concerned with which of the following:

- A. Identify people, groups and organizations that could impact or be impacted by the project.
- B. Communicate and work with the stakeholders to satisfy their needs and expectations
- C. Develop appropriate strategies and an actionable plan to effectively involve stakeholders based on their needs, expectations, and potential impact on the project.
- D. Monitor stakeholder relationships and take appropriate actions as the project evolves and its environment changes

47. Five levels of Stakeholder Engagement are

- A. Unaware, Resistant, Neutral, Supporting, Leading
- B. Unaware, Resilient, Non-committal, Pro-active, Driving
- C. Unknown, Opposing, Neutral, Supporting, Omniscient
- D. Unknown, Resistant, Nebulous, Committed, Lagging

48. The Stakeholder Register is an output of:

- A. Identify Stakeholders
- B. Plan Stakeholder Management
- C. Manage Stakeholder Engagement
- D. Control Stakeholder Engagement

49. All of the following may be considered Enterprise Environmental Factors, EXCEPT:

○ A. Policies and Procedures
○ B. Lessons Learned
○ C. Government Regulations
○ D. Company Holiday Schedule

50. The Project Management Plan describes _____ the project is to be executed, monitored and controlled, and closed.

○ A. Where
○ B. When
○ C. How
○ D. Why

Practice Questions Set #3

50 multiple choice questions

CAPM Knowledge Based Questions

Practice Question Set #3

1. Which project life cycle is intended to respond to high levels of change and ongoing stakeholder involvement:
- A. Predictive
- B. Iterative
- C. Incremental
- D. Adaptive

2. A deliverable is:
- A. a verifiable, measurable work product.
- B. an activity performed by the project team.
- C. an uncertainty that may impact the project.
- D. is a measurement to quantify the amount of variation within a set relative to the mean.

3. Two major categories of influences that can have an impact on a project environment (select 2) :
- ☐ A. Business Case
- ☐ B. Project Benefits Management Plan
- ☐ C. Enterprise Environmental Factors
- ☐ D. Organizational Process Assets
- ☐ E. Project Charter

4. Match the type of power on the left with the correct description from the right column:

____	Formal	1.	Power that comes with the title or position within an organization
____	Expert	2.	Power gained through the ability to provide recognition, monetary, or other desired items
____	Reward	3.	Power earned through the respect for one's experience and education
____	Punitive	4.	Power derived through a connection, or reference to a position of power
____	Referent	5.	Power gained through the ability to invoke discipline or negative consequences

5. A limiting factor that affects the execution of a project, program, or portfolio is known as a:
- ○ A. Product Life Cycle
- ○ B. Constraint
- ○ C. Process
- ○ D. Stakeholder

6. The PMI Talent Triangle defines the qualities & skills of a leader to include which of the following (select 3):
- ☐ A. Seeking Consensus
- ☐ B. Remaining Flexible
- ☐ C. Managing project elements, such as schedule, costs & risks
- ☐ D. Managing relationships and conflicts

7. The majority a project's budget is usually spent during:
- ○ A. Project initiation activities
- ○ B. Project planning activities
- ○ C. Project execution activities
- ○ D. Project closing activities

8. Organizational culture, structure and governance are examples of:
- ○ A. Enterprise Environmental Factors
- ○ B. Stakeholder Engagement Factors
- ○ C. Organizational Process Assets
- ○ D. Organizational Matrix Structures

9. The documented explanation defining the processes for creating, maximizing, and sustaining the benefits of the project is known as:
- ○ A. Project Benefits Management Plan
- ○ B. Project Management Plan
- ○ C. Business Case
- ○ D. Project Charter

Project Management Practice Questions for CAPM & PMP Exams

10. Which of the following become part of the Project Management Plan (select 3):

☐ A. Subsidiary Management Plans (such as Scope Management Plan, Quality Management Plan, etc.)

☐ B. for Scope, Schedule, and Cost

☐ C. Stakeholder Register

☐ E. Risk Register

☐ F. Business Case

11. The project management plan maintains a baseline for all, EXCEPT:

○ A. Scope

○ B. Cost

○ C. Schedule

○ D. Control

12. Which project document is used to link requirements to their origin and track them through all phases of the project life cycle:

○ A. Business Requirement Document

○ B. Requirements Traceability Matrix

○ C. Work Breakdown Structure

○ D. Work Breakdown Dictionary

13. Configuration Management differs from Change Management in that:

○ A. Configuration management controls changes to project activities, while Change management controls all changes impacting project baselines

○ B. Configuration management controls all project level changes, while Change management controls changes affecting the entire organization

○ C. Configuration management controls changes related to product features, while Change management controls all changes impacting project baselines

○ D. Configuration management controls program-level changes, while Change management controls all changes within the portfolio

14. The process of subdividing project deliverables into smaller, more manageable components is Create _____:
- ○ A. Work Breakdown Structure (WBS)
- ○ B. Weighted Scoring Model (WSM)
- ○ C. Work Performance Information (WPI)
- ○ D. Weak Matrix Structure (WMS)

15. Undocumented, unapproved changes to scope is:
- ○ A. Scope Augmentation
- ○ B. Scope Compression
- ○ C. Scope Baseline
- ○ D. Scope Creep

16. Progressive elaboration may continue through the project life cycle, but must adhere to the:
- ○ A. Project configuration statement
- ○ B. Project scope statement
- ○ C. Stakeholder engagement matrix
- ○ D. Requirements traceability matrix

17. The project's deliverables are subdivided so that each project team member has a discreet work package to complete. The work package is:
- ○ A. The lowest level of deliverables decomposition that can be easily assigned, estimated, and managed.
- ○ B. The highest level of deliverables decomposition that can be easily assigned, estimated, and managed.
- ○ C. The lowest level of activity decomposition that can be performed by a single team member.
- ○ D. The highest level of activity decomposition that can be assigned to a functional unit.

18. Which of the following is among the Tools & Techniques of Validate Scope:
- ○ A. Inspection
- ○ B. Detection
- ○ C. Neglection
- ○ D. Selection

19. Validate Scope differs from Control Quality in that:

○ A. Validate Scope is primarily concerned with acceptance of deliverables and meeting product requirements, while Control Quality is concerned with correctness of deliverables and meeting quality requirements.

○ B. Validate Scope is primarily concerned with correctness of deliverables and meeting quality requirements, while Control Quality is concerned with acceptance of deliverables and meeting product requirements.

○ C. Validate Scope is concerned only with Product Scope, while Control Quality is concerned with Project Scope

○ D. Validate Scope is always performed before Control Quality.

20. A Finish-to-Start relationship is an activity relationship that requires the:

○ A. successor be completed before the predecessor may begin.

○ B. successor be completed before the predecessor can finish.

○ C. predecessor be completed before the successor may begin.

○ D. predecessor begins before the successor may begin.

21. A recent project experienced a similar activity taking 12 days to complete. The team now has more experience and can do the work more efficiently, therefore it is estimated at 10 days duration. This is an example of:

○ A. Parkinson's Law

○ B. Analogous Estimating

○ C. Parametric Estimating

○ D. Monte Carlo Technique

Complete the following Critical Path Method Schedule to answer questions #22, #23, and #24:

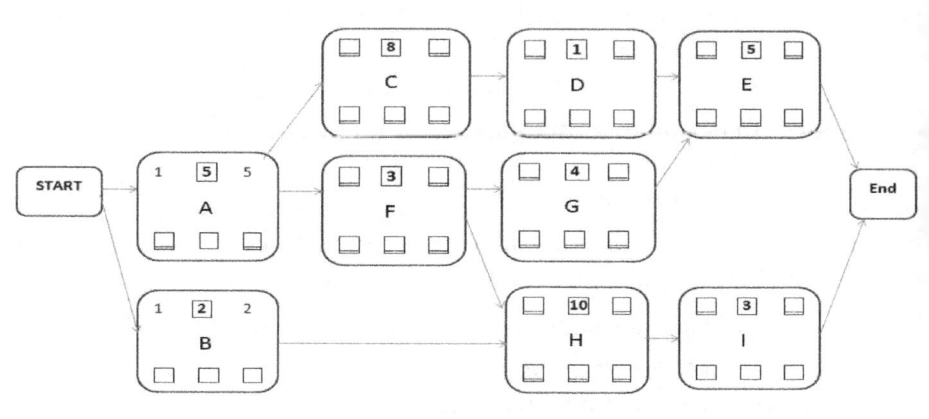

22. Which activity has the most total float:
- A. Activity-A
- B. Activity-B
- C. Activity-C
- D. Activity-D

23. What is the total duration of the critical path:
- A. 16 days
- B. 17 days
- C. 19 days
- D. 21 days

24. Activity-C starts 1 day later than planned, and Activity-D takes 1 day longer to complete than what was originally estimated. How much Float does Activity-E now have?
- A. 3 days
- B. 2 days
- C. 1 day
- D. 0 days

25. The schedule compression technique that adds resources to shorten an activity's duration is known as:
○ A. Crashing
○ B. Fast Tracking
○ C. Slacking
○ D. Rolling Wave

26. You are remodeling your kitchen and have no on-site storage. The appliances must be purchased and delivered by the time the cabinets are completed. This is an example of which dependency relationship:
○ A. Finish-to-Start
○ B. Finish-to-Finish
○ C. Start-to-Start
○ D. Start-to-Finish

27. A Schedule Performance Index (SPI) of less than 1.0 indicates:
○ A. The project is behind schedule.
○ B. The project is under budget.
○ C. The project has experienced a permanent loss of time.
○ D. A project change request must be approved to continue.

28. Project-X has an approved budget of $10,000. Activity-A has a planned value of $500, Activity-B has a planned value of $900, and Activity-C has a planned value of $800. Activities A and B are both complete, but Activity-C is only 75% complete. The actual costs thus far equal $2,500.
The Schedule Variance is _____ , and the schedule status is _____.
○ A. +200 / ahead of schedule
○ B. -200 / behind schedule
○ C. +300 / ahead of schedule
○ D. -300 / behind schedule

Project Management Practice Questions for CAPM & PMP Exams

Use the following Cost Control scenario to answer questions #29 and #30:

> Project-X has an approved budget of $10,000.
> Activity-A has a planned value of $500,
> Activity-B has a planned value of $900, and
> Activity-C has a planned value of $800.
> Activities A and B are both complete, but
> Activity-C is only 75% complete.
> The Actual Costs thus far equal $2,500.

29. The Cost Performance Index (CPI) is _____, and the cost performance is reported to be _____.
    - ○ A. .20 / over budget
    - ○ B. .20 / under budget
    - ○ C. .80 / under budget
    - ○ D. .80 / over budget

30. What is the Estimate at Completion (EAC), assuming that all remaining work is completed according to original estimates:
    - ○ A. $8,900
    - ○ B. $10,200
    - ○ C. $10,500
    - ○ D. $12,500

31. SV, CV, SPI, and CPI are examples of:
    - ○ A. Work Performance Data
    - ○ B. Work Performance Information
    - ○ C. Work Performance Reports
    - ○ D. Work Performance Baselines

32. Which formula is used to forecast the Estimate to Complete (ETC) based on the expectation that cost variances will continue at the same rate as experienced thus far:
    - ○ A. ETC = BAC - EV
    - ○ B. ETC = (BAC - EV)/CPI
    - ○ C. ETC = (BAC - EV)*CPI
    - ○ D. ETC = (BAC - PV)/CPI

Project Management Practice Questions for CAPM & PMP Exams

33. External Failure Costs include the following, EXCEPT:
- ○ A. Liabilities
- ○ B. Warranty Work
- ○ C. Loss of Business
- ○ D. Destructive Testing Loss

34. In quality management, the term 'rework' is considered:
- ○ A. a prevention cost
- ○ B. an internal failure cost
- ○ C. an appraisal cost
- ○ D. a conformance cost

35. Perform Manage Quality differs from Control Quality in that:
- ○ A. Manage Quality is primarily concerned with acceptance of deliverables and meeting product requirements, while Control Quality is concerned with correctness of deliverables and meeting quality requirements.
- ○ B. Manage Quality is primarily concerned with the correctness of deliverables and meeting quality requirements, while Control Quality is concerned with ensuring that appropriate quality standards are used.
- ○ C. Manage Quality is primarily concerned with ensuring that appropriate quality standards are used, while Control Quality is concerned with acceptance of deliverables and meeting product requirements.
- ○ D. Manage Quality is primarily concerned with ensuring that appropriate quality standards are used, while Control Quality is concerned with the correctness of deliverables and meeting quality requirements.

36. To facilitate a problem solving session, the project manager constructs a _____ to conduct root-cause analysis:
- ○ A. Ishikawa, or Fishbone Diagram
- ○ B. Pareto Chart
- ○ C. Gantt Chart
- ○ D. Precedence Diagram

37. Deliverables are _____ of the Control Quality process.
- A. Inputs
- B. Outputs
- C. Tools
- D. Techniques

38. The method of measuring Quality that consists of noting the presence or absence of a specific characteristic while inspecting each deliverable under consideration is known as:
- A. Conformance Sampling
- B. Variables Sampling
- C. Attribute Sampling
- D. Control Sampling

39. There are 16 stakeholders engaged on a project. How many communication channels exist:
- A. 120
- B. 240
- C. 256
- D. 480

40. The Five C's of Communication are comprised of which of the following (select 5):
- ☐ A. Correct Grammar and Spelling
- ☐ B. Concise Expression
- ☐ C. Contradiction and Irrelevance
- ☐ D. Clear Purpose
- ☐ E. Confused Stream of Consciousness
- ☐ F. Coherent Logical Flow
- ☐ G. Controlling Flow of Words and Ideas

41. Non-verbal Communication includes:
- A. Language
- B. Tone
- C. Volume
- D. Body Language

42. The two risk response strategies that can be used for both threats and opportunities are:
- ○ A. Avoid & Accept
- ○ B. Accept & Escalate
- ○ C. Mitigate & Escalate
- ○ D. Exploit & Accept

43. Risk Urgency Assessment considers:
- ○ A. probability factors
- ○ B. impact factors
- ○ C. time factors
- ○ D. category factors

44. Requirements for formal contract acceptance and closure are defined in the:
- ○ A. Proposal
- ○ B. Statement of Work
- ○ C. Procurement Audit
- ○ D. Contract Terms and Conditions

45. Agreements are an output of which Procurement Management process:
- ○ A. Plan Procurement Management
- ○ B. Conduct Procurements
- ○ C. Control Procurements
- ○ D. Close Procurements

46. The Salience Model is used to describe classes of stakeholders based on assessments of (select 3):
- ☐ A. Power
- ☐ B. Urgency
- ☐ C. Neutrality
- ☐ D. Probability
- ☐ E. Legitimacy
- ☐ F. Resistance
- ☐ G. Leadership

47. Match the Contract Type on the left with the appropriate description on the right:

____Firm Fixed Price

1. A hybrid type of contractual arrangement with aspects of both Fixed Price and Cost Reimbursable contracts.

____Fixed Price Incentive Fee

2. The seller is reimbursed for all legitimate project costs incurred, plus a defined payment

____Cost Reimbursable Plus Fixed Fee

3. While the price is set, the buyer and seller agree to financial rewards tied to achieving specific performance objectives stated in the contract.

____Cost Reimbursable Plus Incentive Fee

4. The price for goods is set at the outset and not subject to change, unless the scope of work changes.

____Time and Materials

5. The seller is reimbursed for all legitimate project costs incurred, plus payment based on achieving specific performance objectives stated in the contract.

48. A Bidder Conference is a Tool/Technique of which Procurement process:

- ○ A. Plan Procurement Management
- ○ B. Conduct Procurements
- ○ C. Manage Procurements
- ○ D. Control Procurements

49. The output of Identify Stakeholders is:

○ A. Stakeholder Management Plan
○ B. Stakeholder Register
○ C. Stakeholder Engagement Assessment Matrix
○ D. Work Performance Reports

50. The ability for stakeholders to influence a project is:

○ A. highest during the initial stages and gets progressively lower as the project progresses.
○ B. lowest during the initial stages and gets progressively higher as the project progresses.
○ C. remains constant throughout the project life cycle.
○ D. is driven by the number of influencing stakeholders involved in the project

Project Management Practice Questions for CAPM & PMP Exams

Practice Questions Set #4

50 multiple choice questions

CAPM
Knowledge Based Questions

Practice Question Set #4

1. Which is likely to be part of operations:
○ A. Designing a new engine
○ B. Building a new plant
○ C. Performing scheduled maintenance on a vehicle
○ D. Making updates to reflect changes made to engine specifications

2. A program differs from a portfolio in that:
○ A. a portfolio includes projects, programs and related operational work, while a program consists of related projects.
○ B. a portfolio consists of related projects, while a program consists of unrelated projects.
○ C. a portfolio consists of a collection of large complex projects, while a program consists of smaller simpler projects.
○ D. a portfolio consists of smaller simpler projects, while a program may consist of several portfolios.

3. A Portfolio consists of (select 3)
☐ A. Projects
☐ B. Programs
☐ C. Related operational duties
☐ D. Unapproved project work

4. The PMI Talent Triangle lists Strategic and Business Management as a component of an effective Project Manager's core competencies. Which of the following would be representative of this skill set:
○ A. Building trust and seeking consensus
○ B. Understanding market conditions and time-to-market factors
○ C. Ability to manage project elements, such as schedule, cost, and risk.
○ D. Exhibiting integrity, cultural sensitivity, and courage.

5. Organizational Structures may be defined as (select 3):
- ☐ A. Strong Matrix
- ☐ B. Weak Matrix
- ☐ C. Deep Matrix
- ☐ D. Functional Organization

6. The organization decides to terminate a project. The decision was likely to have been made during:
- ○ A. Stakeholder Engagement Assessment
- ○ B. Phase Gate Review
- ○ C. Project Planning
- ○ D. Qualitative Risk Analysis

7. A change-driven project life cycle is said to be:
- ○ A. Adaptive
- ○ B. Plan Driven
- ○ C. Predictive
- ○ D. Waterfall

8. The meeting where the project manager communicates the objectives of the project, explains the roles and responsibilities of each stakeholder, and obtains the commitment of the project team is called a:
- ○ A. Project Status Meeting
- ○ B. Project Kick-off Meeting
- ○ C. Phase Gate Review
- ○ D. Project Steering Committee Meeting

9. One of the members of the project team has been making unapproved changes to his work, which as a result, affected project scope. This is an example of:
- ○ A. Initiative
- ○ B. Ambiguity
- ○ C. Uncertainty
- ○ D. Scope Creep

Project Management Practice Questions for CAPM & PMP Exams

10. The process Close Project or Phase will yield the following outputs (select 4) :
☐ A. Lessons Learned Register
☐ B. Approval of Project Changes
☐ C. Final Product, Service, or Result Transition
☐ D. Final Report
☐ E. Organizational Process Assets Updates
☐ F. Enterprise Environmental Factor updates

11. Product Scope defines:
○ A. the features and functionality of the project deliverables
○ B. the work necessary to meet stakeholder objectives
○ C. the necessary business information needed to determine whether a project is worth the required investment
○ D. how the project scope will be defined, validated, and controlled.

12. In order for a successor activity to complete, the predecessor must also be complete. This is an example of which type of dependency relationship:
○ A. Finish-to-Finish
○ B. Descretionary
○ C. Start-to-Finish
○ D. Incremental

13. Which of the following statements describe the Critical Path (select 2):
☐ A. Critical path is the shortest total duration from project start to project completion
☐ B. All dependencies on the critical path are discretionary
☐ C. Activities on the critical path have no Lags
☐ D. Activities on the Critical Path have no float
☐ E. Critical path is the longest total duration from project start to project completion

14. Which of the following statements is true:
○ A. Leads and Lags are methods of schedule compression.
○ B. Schedule compression may be mandatory or discretionary.
○ C. Crashing and Fast Tracking are methods of schedule compression.
○ D. Schedule compression may be analogous or parametric.

15. The term used to describe all expected costs predicted to be incurred with the remaining project work is:
- A. Estimate to Complete (ETC)
- B. Estimate at Completion (EAC)
- C. Earned Value Management (EVM)
- D. Expected Monetary Value (EMV)

16. Determine the variance using the factors given in the left column and match to the description of the project status on the right

____	Earned Value = 1,000 Planned Value = 600	1.	Cost Variance = 400 Project is under budget
____	Earned Value = 1,000 Actual Cost = 1,600	2.	Cost Variance = -600 Project is over budget
____	Earned Value = 1,000 Planned Value = 1,600	3.	Schedule Variance = -600 Project is behind schedule
____	Earned Value = 1,000 Actual Cost = 600	4.	Schedule Variance = 400 Project is ahead of schedule

17. A project is 75% complete, but has only expended 50% of its approved budget. The Cost Performance Index (CPI) equals:
- A. 0.67
- B. 1.25
- C. 1.50
- D. 1.75

18. A project has a To-Complete Performance Index (TCPI) = 1.18. Which of the following statements are true (select 2):
- ☐ A. The estimated value of the remaining work exceeds the value of the remaining project funds.
- ☐ B. The project is forcasted to complete under budget
- ☐ C. The project may complete on plan if performance levels improve
- ☐ D. The project is currently behind schedule

19. Quality Metrics are an output of:
○ A. Plan Quality Management
○ B. Manage Quality
○ C. Control Quality
○ D. Release Quality

20. Attribute sampling differs from variables sampling in that:
○ A. attribute sampling is concerned with prevention, while variables sampling is concerned with inspection.
○ B. attribute sampling is concerned with ensuring that appropriate quality standards are used, while variables sampling is concerned with acceptance of deliverables and meeting product requirements.
○ C. attribute sampling is concerned with conformance, while variables sampling is concerned with the degree of conformity.
○ D. attribute sampling is concerned with most common causes, while variables sampling is concerned with root cause analysis.

21. The chart shown below is know as a :

○ A. Flow Chart
○ B. Histogram
○ C. Control Chart
○ D. Scatter Chart

22. Resource Requirements and a Resource Breakdown Structure are outputs of which Project Resource Management process?
○ A. Plan Resource Management
○ B. Estimate Activity Resources
○ C. Acquire Resources
○ D. Control Resources

23. Physical Resource Assignments and Project Team Assignments are outputs of which Project Resource Management process?
- A. Plan Resource Management
- B. Estimate Resources
- C. Acquire Resources
- D. Control Resources

24. Interpersonal and Team Skills include which of the following (select 4):
- A. Benchmarking
- B. Conflict Management
- C. Cultural Awareness
- D. Negotiation
- E. Mind Mapping
- F. Communication

25. Which of the following items are decomposed in a Resource Breakdown Structure (select 3):
- A. Activities
- B. Deliverables
- C. Personnel
- D. Materials
- E. Risks
- F. Equipment

26. Which conflict resolution method results in a 'lose-lose' situation, where both parties must give up something:
- A. Withdraw
- B. Accommodate
- C. Collaborate
- D. Compromise

27. The type of power a project manager received through the approved project charter is referred to as:
- A. Formal
- B. Expert
- C. Reward
- D. Referent

28. The type of power a project manager receives through experience, credibility, and the team's confidence in her leadership is called:
○ A. Formal
○ B. Expert
○ C. Reward
○ D. Referent

29. A project can add specialized expertise without incurring travel or relocation costs when utilizing this type of team:
○ A. Logistical
○ B. Circus
○ C. Virtual
○ D. Co-located

30. The attribute that defines the skills needed to complete the project work is called:
○ A. Confidence
○ B. Contingency
○ C. Co-location
○ D. Competence

31. A project initially starts out with 3 stakeholders, but increases to 7 over the course of the project. How many new communication channels have been added?
○ A. 4
○ B. 15
○ C. 18
○ D. 21

32. A Communications Management Plan should include all of the following, EXCEPT:
○ A. Methods, media, and technologies to be used in communicating project information
○ B. Escalation processes
○ C. Protocols for sensitive/confidential information
○ D. Strategies for responding to positive and negative risks

33. You plan to conduct a Kick-off meeting at which all of the following will be presented, EXCEPT:
- A. Project Scope, Objectives, and Known Risks
- B. Formats and frequencies for project communications
- C. Roles and Responsibilities
- D. Work Performance Information

34. Which of the following is the process of ensuring the information needs of the project and its stakeholders are being met?
- A. Plan Communications Management
- B. Manage Communications
- C. Monitor Communications
- D. Direct Communications

35. Plan Risk Management considers the measurable thresholds of the organization and stakeholders as:
- A. Risk Appetite
- B. Risk Reward
- C. Risk Avoidance
- D. Risk Mitigation

36. Probability differs from Impact in that:
- A. Probability is the likelihood that a risk event will occur, while Impact is the likelihood that it will not occur.
- B. Probability is the likelihood that a risk event will occur, while Impact is its effect on scope, schedule, and cost.
- C. Probability is the effect that a risk event will have on scope, schedule, and cost, while Impact is the likelihood that it will occur.
- D. Probability is concerned with risk urgency, while Impact is concerned with risk aversion.

37. A risk is identified that may cost the project an additional $12,000 if it occurs, but there is only a 5% chance that it will occur. The Expected Monetary Value (EMV) calculated for contingency reserve is:
- A. $12,000
- B. $11,400
- C. $6,000
- D. $600

38. The project team identifies a potential opportunity, however cannot exploit it due to schedule constraints on project work. You provide this response strategy as an option to the project sponsor:
- A. Avoid
- B. Share
- C. Transfer
- D. Mitigate

39. Contingency Reserves differ from Management Reserves in that:
- A. Contingency Reserves are not part of the project cost baseline, while Management Reserves are included in the cost baseline.
- B. Contingency Reserves require change approval to be expended, while Management Reserves are can be utilized without change approval.
- C. Contingency Reserves are established for future situations that can be planned for in part, while Management Reserves are established for future situations that are impossible to predict.
- D. Contingency Reserves are established for situations that have already occurred, while Management Reserves are established to deal with situations that may occur in the future.

40. An opportunity is identified to have a 40% chance of earning $200,000, but there is a 20% chance that it can lose $40,000. What is the total Expected Monetary Value (EMV) of the risk:
- A. $160,000
- B. $80,000
- C. $72,000
- D. $40,000

41. Make-or-Buy Decision is among the Outputs of which Project Procurement Management process
- A. Plan Procurement Management
- B. Conduct Procurements
- C. Control Procurements
- D. Close Procurements

42. A Bidder Conference is among the Tools & Techiques of which Project Procurement Management process

○ A. Plan Procurement Management
○ B. Conduct Procurements
○ C. Manage Procurements
○ D. Control Procurements

43. The contract type with the lowest risk for the buyer is:

○ A. Fixed Price
○ B. Cost Reimbursable
○ C. Time and Materials
○ D. Compensatory

44. The buyer's description of the work or product being procured is known as a:

○ A. Request for Information
○ B. Request for Proposal
○ C. Terms and Conditions
○ D. Statement of Work

45. All of the following behaviors can build and sustain credibility with project stakeholders, EXCEPT:

○ A. Being flexible and open to new ideas
○ B. Being respectful
○ C. Being quick to judge and unapologetic
○ D. Being reliable and committed

46. The modeling technique that describes stakeholder's influence based on assessments of their power (ability to influence the outcomes of the project), urgency (their need for immediate attention), and involvement is known as:

○ A. Stakeholder Rubric
○ B. Salience Model
○ C. Tornado Diagram
○ D. Tuckman's Ladder

47. A stakeholder withholds information that is key to achieving project objectives. This stakeholder is said to be:

○ A. Unaware
○ B. Resistant
○ C. Storming
○ D. Salient

48. Match the level of Stakeholder Engagement on the left with the appropriate description in the right column:

_____	Unaware	1.	Aware of the project, but participating at a bare minimum level
_____	Resistant	2.	Uses power and resources within their control to ensure the success of the project
_____	Neutral	3.	Does not know about the project and potential impacts
_____	Supportive	4.	Unsupportive of the work or outcomes of the project
_____	Leading	5.	Actively engaged in the project

49. Which of the following statements is true:

○ A. Stakeholder engagement may change over the project life cycle.
○ B. Stakeholder engagement is equal to the power held within the organization.
○ C. Stakeholder engagement is constant throughout the project life cycle.
○ D. Stakeholder engagement is highest at project initiation and decreases over the course of the project.

50. The ability of a stakeholder to influence the project is:

○ A. Highest at project initiation and decreases over the project life cycle.
○ B. Lowest at project initiation and increases over the project life cycle.
○ C. Constant throughout the project life cycle.
○ D. Low until deliverables are inspected, then increases sharply.

Practice Questions Set #5

50 multiple choice questions

PMP Situational Questions

Practice Question Set #5

1. You learn that the vendor selected for your project was late in delivering in a similar situation on two previous projects. You decide to _____ the risk by going with a different vendor.
- A. Mitigate
- B. Assume
- C. Accept
- D. Avoid

2. Jaime is managing a project for an organization that produces equipment used in health care facilities. The project deliverables are considered to be of a high grade, and the organization is prepared to fund the project sufficiently to deliver a high level of quality. Which of the following is not included in the cost of quality?
- A. Prevention Costs
- B. Maintenance Costs
- C. Appraisal Costs
- D. Failure Costs

3. You are the project manager in a multi-national organization. How can you best prevent misunderstandings due to cross-cultural differences?
- A. Use all appropriate methods of communications and follow up in writing when communicating verbally. Remember that cultural diversity may help project teams solve unforeseen problems over the course of the project.
- B. Keep in mind that some cultures are more developed than others. Some have strong values, while some do not. Therefore you should avoid choosing members from countries with cultures that are not similar to your own.
- C. Since communication habits differ significantly across various cultures, communicating between people from different countries should only be limited to verbal. The use of non-verbal communications bears too many risks.
- D. Cultural differences can prevent a project from being successful. Project teams should be fully assimilated to ensure that cultural differences do not disrupt the work.

4. You find that a rejected change request was implemented by the project team, who knew of the change request but not of the rejection. In order to avoid such a situation, rejected change requests should be consistently communicated to stakeholders through which process?
- ○ A. Define Scope
- ○ B. Manage Quality
- ○ C. Plan Stakeholder Engagement
- ○ D. Perform Integrated Change Control

5. You are advised that it is a customary practice in one of your project locations to tip the delivery persons 5% of the value of the materials delivered. This is the case in your other locations, not is it customary in your home office location. You should
- ○ A. Refuse to tip the delivery person
- ○ B. Include the same 5% tip to delivery persons in your other locations
- ○ C. Tip the delivery person as is customary for the location
- ○ D. Tip an amount less than the customary 5%

6. You are managing a project to satisfy compliance requirements for a conservative financial services company. You understand that precautions must be taken to avoid jeopardizing project completion. The Risk Management Plan should indicate the organization's:
- ○ A. Risk Reward
- ○ B. Risk Register
- ○ C. Risk Appetite
- ○ D. Risk Urgency

7. The project manager's role during the Conduct Procurements process is:
- ○ A. to make the Make-or-Buy decision
- ○ B. to ensure project risks are understood
- ○ C. to establish source selection criteria
- ○ D. to approve changes to the agreement

Project Management Practice Questions for CAPM & PMP Exams

8. You prepare a project management plan, a project schedule, and a risk register. These project documents should be distributed to
○ A. All people assigned to activities
○ B. All people identified in Communications Management Plan
○ C. All people identified in the Stakeholder Register
○ D. All people identified in the RACI chart as accountable

9. During proof of concept testing, an engineer discovers that using a slightly larger cylinder will improve the product's efficiency. There would be no impact on cost and schedule baselines, and key stakeholders agree to proceed on the engineer's recommendation. How should this be recorded?
○ A. In accordance with the Quality Management Plan
○ B. As an opportunity in the Risk Register
○ C. As a revision to the Scope Statement
○ D. Within the product's Configuration Controls

10. A change is identified in order to bring future performance in line with the Project Management Plan. This is know as:
○ A. Preventive action
○ B. Corrective action
○ C. Quantitative action
○ D. Defect repair

11. An upcoming activity is estimated as 3 days work. When placing an order on Monday, March 19 for the required supplies, you are told that delivery will be in 4 days. Your team is not approved to work overtime or weekends, therefore you schedule the work for:
○ A. March 29 - 31
○ B. March 23 - 25
○ C. March 20 - 22
○ D. March 23 - 27

12. An installer tells you that he cannot complete the installation until power to the work site is upgraded. This is reflected in the project schedule as which type of dependency?

○ A. Discretionary
○ B. Referential
○ C. Preferential
○ D. Mandatory

13. In order to meet regulatory requirements, the scheduled completion date of your project must be brought in by 2 weeks. You immediately begin to

○ A. Forecast the Estimate At Completion (EAC)
○ B. Determine Contingency Reserves
○ C. Review the Critical Path for activities that can be expedited
○ D. Crash activities with the longest duration estimates

14. After completing your project schedule, you learn that Philip, a key resource, has resigned from the organization. You are advised by management that Philip's position will not be replaced, nor will additional funds for contract labor be authorized.

Two individuals on the project team have the competencies to complete Philip's work, however both are already assigned to activities in this phase. You revise the project schedule to reflect:

○ A. Resource Leveling to create a resource constrained project schedule
○ B. Fast Tracking of all activities being reassigned
○ C. External Dependencies resulting from the removal of a key resource
○ D. Critical Chain Method (CCM) instead of Critical Path Method (CPM)

15. Given the following costs:
   Concept = $3,000
   Design = $7,000
   Development = $36,000
   Testing = $4,000
   Training = $ 2,000
   Maintenance = $4,000
What is the total project life cycle cost?
- A. $47,000
- B. $50,000
- C. $52,000
- D. $56,000

16. Sara is managing a project for Wheezer Technologies, in which the Cost Management Plan defines a variance threshold of +/- 10%. This means
- A. Cost Variance (CV) of -$5,000 on a $50,000 project is considered to be "on plan"
- B. Schedule Variance (SV) of +$10,000 on a $100,000 project is considered to be "over budget"
- C. Seven consecutive occurrences greater than 10% of mean, or less than 10% of the mean constitutes an "out of control" process
- D. Cost Performance Indicator (CPI) of 10% or more will indicate a "cost overrun"

17. A work package was estimated to cost $2,000 and finish today, but instead it has incurred a cost of $1,600 and only three-fourths complete, The Cost Variance is
- A. +100
- B. -400
- C. -100
- D. +400

18. Your project sponsor has emphasized the need for cost controls. To address these concerns, you should provide:
- A. Earned Value Performance Measurements
- B. Control Charts
- C. Work Performance Data
- D. Disbursement Detail Reports

19. You are preparing a monthly project status which includes a budget forecast. You decide to adjust the estimate for remaining project work by the Cost Performance Index (CPI) to determine Estimate To Complete (ETC) because:

○ A. Original estimates are found to be unreliable and unpredictable

○ B. Original estimates are found to be accurate, but took longer than expected to complete

○ C. Current Variances are viewed as typical of future variances

○ D. Current Variances are viewed as atypical and isolated to past activities that have already completed

20. You are managing a software development project for a customer that provided their guidelines on data security, redundancy, and archival. These are documented as:

○ A. Non-Functional Requirements

○ B. Business Requirements

○ C. Transitional Requirements

○ D. Functional Requirements

21. After meeting with subject matter experts, it is clear that some aspects of the product are well defined, while other aspects require more research and analysis to finalize. You recommend:

○ A. Postponing the project until all requirements are fleshed out thoroughly

○ B. Eliminating the items that require more analysis from the Scope Statement

○ C. Defining a strong, but adaptable Scope Statement and use the concept of progressive elaboration to allow product specifications to evolve.

○ D. Defining an intentionally vague Scope Statement so that progressive elaboration can be utilized to include any and all future requirements.

22. During product testing, your engineers advise you that defects are found as speed is accelerates and the temperature rises. You ask that the specific data points are prepared for presentation to key stakeholders in the form of a:
- A. Histogram
- B. Pareto Chart
- C. Flow Chart
- D. Scatter Diagram

23. A project is initiated to address new product safety requirements recently signed into law. The business case states the key objective for the project is:
- A. Cost/Benefit
- B. Legal/Compliance
- C. Customer/Request
- D. Critical Path

24. Francis is managing a project to remodel a museum in Tucumcari, New Mexico. Using earned value management, he figures out that the project is currently on schedule but $1,200 over budget. Which aspect of the PMI Talent Triangle has been illustrated in this example:
- A. Strategic and Business Management
- B. Financial Management
- C. Technical Project Management
- D. Earned Value Management

25. Several team members disagree on a design approach. You recognize the importance of not only a good design choice, but also consensus toward a joint decision. You encourage:
- A. Compromise
- B. Competence
- C. Collaboration
- D. Co-location

26. In the days following project kick-off, you notice several team members doing work not assigned to them, while other team members with subject matter expertise are not being included in requirements analysis. You immediately
- ○ A. Reconvene the entire team for another kickoff meeting
- ○ B. Prepare a Pareto chart and distribute to key stakeholders
- ○ C. Report these activities to the Project Sponsor
- ○ D. Prepare a RACI chart and distribute for immediate attention

27. Although project reports are provided on a regular basis to senior management, there is a perception that the organization's decision makers are not aware of risks that may endanger project success. You choose to
- ○ A. Improve hierarchical focus, specifically upward
- ○ B. Increase the frequency of project reports
- ○ C. Emphasize the external focus of project reports
- ○ D. Utilize the bottom-up method of communication

28. You observe 7 consecutive measurements on a control chart recorded between the mean and the lower control limit. This indicates the process to be:
- ○ A. Stable and Sustainable
- ○ B. Unstable, due to Special Causes
- ○ C. Unstable, due to Common Causes
- ○ D. Stable, but not SustainableQuestion #29

29. Claire's assignment cannot begin until the completion of 3 separate predecessor activities. The probability of each of these activities completing on schedule is as follows:
   Activity-A : 75%
   Activity-B : 90%
   Activity-C : 95%

The probability of Claire starting her assignment on time is
- ○ A. 95%
- ○ B. 90%
- ○ C. 86%
- ○ D. 64%

Project Management Practice Questions for CAPM & PMP Exams

30. In an effort to compress project schedule, you crash an activity estimated at 21 days duration by increasing the number of resources from 4 to 12. You are surprised to find the activity still took 14 days to complete. This may have been a result of:
- A. The law of diminishing returns
- B. The rule of seven
- C. The 80/20 rule
- D. The Delphi factor

31. When is a stakeholder's ability to influence the direction of a project greatest?
- A. As the project nears completion
- B. When the budget is depleted
- C. Just prior to conducting product inspections
- D. During project initiation

32. Mid-way through project execution, you receive a letter to cease and desist. It seems that a key product design constitutes an infringement on a competitor's patent. This was never thought to be in violation, nor identified as a project risk; therefore, no contingencies were established. A consultant was contacted to provide an alternative, which while feasible would require additional budget. As project manager, you should:
- A. Stop all project activities and initiate project closure
- B. Utilize your contingency reserve to proceed with the consultant's alternative
- C. Initiate a change request for the appropriation of management reserves to fund the consultant's alternative
- D. Record the patent infringement on the Risk Register, along with its probability, impact and urgency

33. Managing a virtual team increases the importance of the
- A. Cost Management Plan
- B. Scope Management Plan
- C. Communications Management Plan
- D. Risk Management Plan

34. The project sponsor advises you that all company projects are being cut by 10% of their budget, which equals $17,500 reduction in your cost baseline. You should:

○ A. Make an entry in the Risk Register and work with your project team to determine probability, impact, and urgency

○ B. Review the Critical Path Method (CPM) for activities that can be crashed

○ C. Forecast an Estimate To Completion (ETC) and work with your project team to propose alternatives for stakeholder approval that will align future activities with the revised budget

○ D. Review the Work Breakdown Structure (WBS) with key stakeholders to reduce the cost of each work package by 10%

35. After a vendor was awarded a contract on your project, the account manager presents you with a set of golf clubs as a gift and invites you to a golf outing. You should

○ A. Accept it, since refusal may insult the vendor

○ B. Accept it, since the contract has already been awarded therefore would not influence your selection

○ C. Decline tactfully, as acceptance may be viewed as an inappropriate personal gain

○ D. Refuse it, and terminate the contract with the vendor due to inappropriate behavior on the part of the account manager

36. You discover that a new technology was utilized by your team, allowing them to complete their activities in half the estimated time. You should:

○ A. Calculate the positive Schedule Variance (SV) and offer the customer a refund

○ B. Document as Lessons Learned so future projects can achieve similar performance

○ C. Record the opportunity on the Risk Register to offset contingency reserves calculated for threats

○ D. Use the newly found time to deliver additional unapproved scope

37. Which of the following is conducted to identify inefficient and ineffective policies and procedures used by a project?
- A. Quality Audit
- B. Quality Inspection
- C. Quality Benchmarking
- D. Quality Control

38. George notices that the engineering team is not attending monthly status meetings, only to discover the appointments were sent to an obsolete email address. George fixes this as part of the:
- A. Identify Stakeholders process
- B. Plan Communications Management process
- C. Monitor Communications process
- D. Plan Stakeholder Engagement process

39. You read an article in a trade publication providing academic research that supports a shift in the cultural and political climate in some emerging markets. These new market conditions influence your project as:
- A. Enterprise Environmental Factors (EEFs) internal to the organization
- B. Enterprise Environmental Factors (EEFs) external to the organization
- C. Operational Process Assets (OPAs) internal to the organization
- D. Operational Process Assets (OPAs) external to the organization

40. Team members respect Rakesh for his experience and project management knowledge, and trust that he knows how to handle issues. This describes
- A. Expert power
- B. Legitimate power
- C. Referent power
- D. Representative power

41. After reading customer reviews of a competitor's product, a key stakeholder requests that additional performance tests be performed prior to market launch. This represents a change to

○ A. Product scope
○ B. Business Requirements
○ C. Business Case
○ D. Project Scope

42. You find out that a professional printer can produce and mail brochures faster and at a lower cost than your company can do in-house. By choosing the printer, you've made a:

○ A. Parametric Decision
○ B. Analogous Decision
○ C. Make or Buy Decision
○ D. Fast Track Decision

43. While there is no single "best method" for dealing with conflict, one method is considered least effective since it doesn't really resolve the conflict

○ A. Smooth
○ B. Force
○ C. Withdrawal
○ D. Compromise

44. A Break-Even point is presented in the Business Case. You define how this will be achieved and measured in the:

○ A. Cost Management Plan
○ B. Statement of Work
○ C. Project Management Plan
○ D. Project Benefits Management Plan

45. You contract an engineering firm to design a critical component of the project's key deliverable, which will then be built by your company's internal development team. What document is used to ensure all requirements are captured in the design, and built into the end product?
- A. Scope Statement
- B. Traceability Matrix
- C. Gantt Chart
- D. Stakeholder Engagement Matrix

46. You are approved for additional budget to expedite project delivery, so you lease a piece of equipment that can be used to reduce Activity-X, a critical path activity, by 4 days. Activity-Y is a start-to-start successor to Activity-X and has 3 days float.
Which of the following statements best describes the result of this change?
- A. Activity-X is being fast tracked, and the project will complete 4 days earlier than originally scheduled.
- B. Activity-X is being crashed, and the project will complete 3 days earlier than originally scheduled.
- C. Activity-Y will now have an additional 4 days float
- D. Both activities are now planned for completion at exactly the same time

47. With several activities significantly behind schedule, you advise the project sponsor that factors external to the project team's control will inhibit the ability to catch up. The sponsor understands, and asks you to meet with a key stakeholder to consider a new requirement that she insists must be included in the project. Which of the following processes will require your immediate attention?
- A. Control Schedule
- B. Perform Integrated Change Control
- C. Control Scope
- D. Perform Qualitative Risk Analysis

48. A developer on your e-commerce project provides an estimate of 12 days to complete an assignment. She is fairly confident in her estimate, and doesn't expect any issues; however, she advises that if there is a problem that requires vendor support the duration could easily double. You ask if there is any chance it could be completed earlier, to which she replied 'not likely.'
You choose to use the _____ method to estimate the activity's duration at _____ days.
- ○ A. Three-Point Triangular / 14 days
- ○ B. Three-Point Beta / 14 days
- ○ C. Three-Point Beta / 16 days
- ○ D. Parametric / 18 days

49. An Request For Proposal (RFP) has been sent to four candidate vendors. One vendor contacts you during the response period and asks for clarification on a vague specification. You should
- ○ A. Answer the vendor's question verbally
- ○ B. Answer the vendor's question in writing
- ○ C. Provide written clarification to all four candidate vendors
- ○ D. Refuse to answer any questions during the response period

50. Adrian is managing the rollout of a new Point of Sale (POS) system to the company's 18 store locations. Since the work for each location will be similar, Adrian conforms to this type of project life cycle
- ○ A. Presumptive
- ○ B. Iterative
- ○ C. Predictive
- ○ D. Adaptive

Project Management Practice Questions for CAPM & PMP Exams

Practice Questions Set #6

50 multiple choice questions

PMP
Situational Questions

Practice Question Set #5

1. Who has the authority to request a change to product scope?
- ○ A. Project Sponsor
- ○ B. Project Manager
- ○ C. Product Owner
- ○ D. Any Stakeholder

2. In meeting with a client, you indicate that your firm has successfully completed similar projects with other clients three times in the past 18 months, and that it has taken about 4 weeks to complete the discovery phase. This is an example of:
- ○ A. Analogous Estimate
- ○ B. Parametric Estimate
- ○ C. Three Point Estimate
- ○ D. Past Lives Transgressions

3. Jennifer is the project manager of the ALIANC project within the Altak Communications Corporation. She has worked with the project stakeholders to create an initial scope statement a month ago, but in the time since the scope has evolved and there are more details known. This evolution of scope definition is known as:
- ○ A. Decomposition
- ○ B. Scope Creep
- ○ C. Progressive Elaboration
- ○ D. Critical Path Method

4. Your subject matter expert advises you that four distinct tasks must be completed in order to produce a work package that is integral to meeting product scope requirements. This represents:
- ○ A. Critical Path Method
- ○ B. Precedence Diagram Method
- ○ C. Define Activities process
- ○ D. Sequence Activities process

5. The Dunston Jacoby Corporation is rebranding itself as the DJC and creating a new company logo. All projects, as well as operational work, associated with this initiative will be tracked and managed in a coordinated way because of its reflection of the overall corporate image. This is an example of a:

○ A. Project
○ B. Program
○ C. Portfolio
○ D. Primus

6. You are managing of a showroom renovation project and recognize that you and your team have a lot of experience executing similar projects, and that your organization has a wealth of Organizational Process Assets.

You've worked with your team to define the work involved and have a very detailed Work Breakdown Structure. You decide to employ the services of a contractor for all defined electrical work. What type of a contract would you prefer to use?

○ A. Cost Reimbursable
○ B. Fixed Price
○ C. Service Level Agreement
○ D. Time and Material

7. You are assigned to work with another PMP on a complex, multi-faceted project. You've heard from one team member that this other project manager's practices are often in violation of the PMI Code of Ethics and Professional Conduct. What should you do next?

○ A. Discuss your concerns with the project sponsor
○ B. Report the violations to the organization's human resources department
○ C. Assess the credibility of the accusations before taking any action
○ D. Do nothing since the project manager is not under your direct authority

8. Shawn is managing a financial services project for a large brokerage organization. He knows from doing Variance Analysis that the project is currently ahead of schedule and over budget. In order to determine the rate at which the remaining work must be performed to close the project within the approved Cost Baseline, Shawn calculates the:

○ A. Internal Rate of Return (IRR)
○ B. To-Complete Performance Index (TCPI)
○ C. Schedule Performance Index (SPI)
○ D. Enterprise Environmental Factor (EEF)

9. Bernard has been assigned to manage a software development project, and is working with his team to sequence activities.

The solution architect, Dolores, indicates that rather than performing a resource intensive process immediately upon request, a workflow queue should be introduced to prioritize requests, and process them according to priority. The development of the workflow queue should precede solution testing.

This dependency would be considered as :

○ A. Mandatory
○ B. Systemic
○ C. Expert
○ D. Discretionary

10. You've obtained three estimates to complete a task. The optimistic is 3 days, the pessimistic is 15 days, and the most likely is 12 days. You choose the Beta (weighted average) method of 3-point Estimating and schedule the task for a duration of:

○ A. 9 days
○ B. 10 days
○ C. 11 days
○ D. 12 days

11. Marisol is managing the development of a security system, that involves the use of a new, state-of-the-art technology. Marisol is facing problems decomposing the 'System Test' work package and defining the final activities required to complete the work package.

What is the best way to resolve this problem?

○ A. Use a Waterfall approach to decompose 'System Development' work packages, and an Agile approach to decompose the 'System Test' work package

○ B. Use a Rolling Wave approach to decompose the System Development work packages now, and decompose the System Test work package later, when more details become available.

○ C. Consult your Project Management Plan to determine what to do in this situation.

○ D. Use the Analogous approach to decompose the System Test work package as it was done on a previous project.

12. Tanya is managing a waste management project and understands that work may not begin before obtaining a government environmental agency's permit. It is not known how long it will take to receive the permit, but rumored to be several months. The milestone schedule is aggressive and penalties may be incurred if missed.

Obtaining this work permit is an example of :

○ A. Internal Dependency
○ B. External Dependency
○ C. Cost Reimbursement plus Fee
○ D. Cost Reimbursement plus Incentive

13. After issuing an 'on schedule' status to your project sponsor and stakeholders, a team member informs you that they provided you with an incorrect date. The impact of correcting this error now places the project behind schedule. You should:

○ A. Discuss the termination of the team member with his immediate supervisor.

○ B. Let the stakeholders know the report was incorrect, and provide them with current status.

○ C. Wait until the next reporting cycle to correct the error.

○ D. Reward the team member for being so brave and honest to admit to her mistake.

Project Management Practice Questions for CAPM & PMP Exams

14. You've just learned that a team member, Marco, has been pulled by the CEO to perform a special assignment. Marco's project work is identified as having 4 days float. You should first:

○ A. Find out if the CEO's special assignment is expected to take 4 days or less.
○ B. Advise the CEO that the project's final deliverable will be delayed by the 4 days necessary for Marco to complete his special assignment
○ C. Reassign all of Marco's project work to another resource
○ D. Deny the CEO access to your project team resources.

15. All construction projects performed in the Metro area within the past two years have experienced cost overruns averaging 12% of total budget. You are assigned a similar project and advise your project sponsor to:

○ A. Maintain a Management Reserve, that will be requisitioned via a change request only if needed.
○ B. Maintain a Management Reserve as part of the Cost Baseline designated for unforeseen circumstances.
○ C. Maintain a Contingency Reserve as part of the Cost Baseline designated for unforeseen circumstances.
○ D. Increase all Cost Estimates prepared by the team by 12%.

16. Jon's company secured a large system development contract and assigned him as the project manager. The project work has been going smoothly, and the customer has been delighted with both the quality of the work that has been completed and Jon's leadership of the project team.

In fact, they are planning to have even more project work next year, and Jon's senior management realizes that this client could drive more business to their firm.

Since the future project work is not yet certain, Jon considers it to be a:

○ A. Threat
○ B. Reserve
○ C. Opportunity
○ D. Contingency

Project Management Practice Questions for CAPM & PMP Exams

17. Pavel is a project manager working in a fast-paced consumer electronics company. The key objectives of the project are constrained by a fixed deadline, in which the product's market launch must coincide with the Holiday season. To maximize the value of the product's features within the given timeframe, Pavel decides to utilize:
- A. Fast Track Life Cycle
- B. Agile Life Cycle
- C. Predictive Life Cycle
- D. Critical Path Life Cycle

18. Lois calculates the SPI to be 0.86. This means:
- A. for every dollar spent the project has earned 86 cents worth of value
- B. the project has spent 86 cents for every dollar of value earned thus far.
- C. the project has completed 86% of the work planned thus far
- D. the project is 86% ahead of schedule

19. Okechuku is halfway through project execution and the project is expected to go for another 11 months. He thinks that things are going as per plan. Mara, the project sponsor has asked for a project performance report to be presented during next status meeting.

Okechuku performs Variance Analysis to find that the Actual Cost is more than the Earned Value, and the Planned Value is less than the Earned Value. What would be the interpretation of this data?
- A. The project is over budget and behind schedule
- B. The project is over budget but ahead of schedule
- C. The project is within budget but behind schedule
- D. The project is within budget and ahead of schedule

20. Yolanda is managing a pharmaceutical project, where the nature of work is very complex and involves a lot of research.

Both the development team and testing team suggest that the Taguchi method be used as a Design of Experiments. While this is time consuming, the team recommends this approach will add necessary controls and will lead to a better quality of deliverables.

What is the best course of action?
- A. Start using the Taguchi method immediately, since the changes will help improve quality and the team agrees this to be the appropriate method.
- B. Analyze the benefits of implementing the Taguchi method as well as the impact on project cost and schedule, then write up a Change Request for stakeholder approval.
- C. Refuse to implement this change as it would represent a departure from the agreed upon testing methodology.
- D. Study the benefits vs. costs, and authorize the additional work if it proves to be a cost effective opportunity.

21. You are involved in a project for manufacturing widgets. You notice that the quality of the widgets being produced has deviated from the parameters specified in project management plan. In order to bring it in line with the specifications, you initiate :
- A. Corrective Action
- B. Risk Analysis
- C. Defect Repair
- D. Preventive Action

22. Your project deliverables did not meet quality requirements desired by your customer. As a result, some of your products were rejected and there is a possibility that you would not receive repeat business from the customer. From a quality perspective, the costs associated with the rejected products can be categorized:
- A. Appraisal Costs
- B. Customer Retention Costs
- C. External Failure Costs
- D. Performance Costs

23. The project you are managing requires a large component of the project team to be involved in the planning processes. You decide to hold the Kick-off Meeting:
- A. Shortly after project approval
- B. Just prior to project execution
- C. As soon as all known project risks have been resolved
- D. During project transition

24. Your project is 60% complete and $75,000 of the $100,000 budget has been spent. What is the cost performance required to be achieved to finish the remaining work within budget?
- ○ A. 0.8
- ○ B. 1.4
- ○ C. 1.6
- ○ D. 1.8

25. Your company policy defines a specific limit on the value of gifts you can award to customers in a year. By mistake, you award a second gift to a customer's representative which is now beyond the annual limit mentioned in your company policy.
What should you do?
- ○ A. Do Nothing; the policy is just a guideline to prevent abuse.
- ○ B. Call the customer and ask him return one of the gifts.
- ○ C. Contact your manager to discuss your mistake.
- ○ D. Resign from the organization in shame.

26. You see a need to establish a time frame that a service provider will respond to issues from your organization, based on the severity level of the issue being reported. A contract that would govern such activity is known as:
- ○ A. Purchase Order
- ○ B. Unilateral Agreement
- ○ C. Indemnification
- ○ D. Service Level Agreement

27. You are in the process of leading a project team to perform the work defined in the project management plan, and to implement approved changes to achieve the project`s objectives. This is done during:
- ○ A. Direct and Manage Project Work
- ○ B. Develop Project Management Plan
- ○ C. Monitor and Control Project Work
- ○ D. Manage Project Knowledge

28. Your organization is evaluating whether to renovate an existing 1,000 seat theater at a cost of $5 million, or to build a new theater with 75% greater seating capacity at a cost of $12 million.

Business planners estimate the probability of a strong demand for tickets at 60% for sold-out shows, and 40% for half-capacity. Ticket prices and number of performances per year are assumed equal in both scenarios: $100 per seat & 200 performances per year.

Using Decision Tree Analysis, how would you aid the organization in decision support?

○   A. Building the new theater requires a greater investment, but returns a greater Expected Monetary Value

○   B. Renovating the existing theater requires a greater investment, but returns a greater Expected Monetary Value

○   C. Building the new theater requires a lower investment, but returns a greater Expected Monetary Value

○   D. Renovating the existing theater requires a lower investment, but returns a greater Expected Monetary Value

29. During Risk Analysis, Brigitte employs the use of Monte Carlo simulation to understand the level of uncertainty in the variables contributing to a specific risk. The results of the current simulation differs from the results of the initial simulation performed 6 weeks earlier at project start because:

○   A. As the project work progressed, some uncertainties have been eliminated while others have materialized as issues, thereby changing the overall level of uncertainty.

○   B. The simulation was run in error leading to different results.

○   C. The level of uncertainty is always expected to increase as project work progresses.

○   D. Monte Carlo simulations can only be performed once during a project's life cycle.

30. The project team has successfully delivered the final component of a year long project on-budget and ahead of schedule. The final product has been transitioned into operations and all necessary support requirements have been completed. As part of project closure, what would be done next?

○ A. Release all project resources
○ B. Validate Scope
○ C. Complete project closure documents
○ D. Close out all project accounts

31. The project sponsor provides you with a brief overview of a new project for you to manage. It is a result your company being selected through a long RFP evaluation by the customer, and being awarded the contract.

You decide to create a Project Charter for your sponsor to review and approve, however you soon realize his overview did not provide enough information. What would be you best course of action?

○ A. Prepare the Project Charter with the just the information provided
○ B. Ask your sponsor to provide all missing information
○ C. Contact the customer to provide you with the RFP, Statement of Work, and signed agreements pertaining to the project
○ D. Skip the Project Charter phase, and initiate project planning.

32. Your project requires two different grades of a similar material, the higher grade for exposed surfaces and the lower grade for non-visible purposes. These materials are listed on the:

○ A. Activity List
○ B. Resource Breakdown Structure
○ C. RACI Chart
○ D. Quality Breakdown Structure

33. You are the project manager in a manufacturing firm that produces machine parts required in automobile production. During a milestone review, you discover some design requirements have not taken into account. You should:
○ A. Stop all project activities and initiate project closure
○ B. Inform your project sponsor that the project will be delayed because of the missed requirements.
○ C. Instruct your team to incorporate the requirements and do an analysis to figure out the potential impact.
○ D. Go ahead with production because incorporating the requirements may delay the schedule.

34. Which of the following types of costs is NOT incurred toward ensuring conformance to requirements?
○ A. Warranty Costs
○ B. Inspection Cost
○ C. Training Cost
○ D. Equipment Cost

35. Charles notices that the project team has been working together for a while, but not yet open towards collaboration. He decides to engage the group in team building activities to move the stage of team development from :
○ A. Forming to Storming
○ B. Storming to Norming
○ C. Norming to Performing
○ D. Storming to Performing

36. After a week of meetings, no progress has been made to reach a project decision. It seems two departments are at odds over which will have responsibilty for performing a particular activity. You engage the project sponsor to review the details and make a binding decision. This is an example of:
○ A. Expert Power
○ B. Project Charter Authority
○ C. Force/Direct Conflict Resolution
○ D. Stakeholder Engagement Matrix

37. Which of the following statements about Scope is true:
- ○ A. Project Scope is more important than Product Scope
- ○ B. Project Scope is measured against the Project Management Plan, while Produce Scope is measured against the Requirements
- ○ C. Project Scope is initiated in the Project Charter, while Product Scope is initiated in the Project Management Plan
- ○ D. Project Scope is more vulnerable to scope creep than Product Scope

38. Mind Mapping:
- ○ A. Requires specialized training and certification to administer, and a signed liability release from each participant.
- ○ B. Traces each requirement through each phase of the project life cycle to ensure that none are forgotten
- ○ C. Is a repository used in the Agile project framework to collect requirements for estimation, prioritization, and selection for an increment.
- ○ D. Consolidates ideas from individual brainstorming sessions into a single map to reflect commonality and differences in understanding, and to generate new ideas,

39. Francoise is advised that the network equipment and peripherals have specific temperature and humidity requirements for their operation. To ensure the data center meets these requirements, she schedules a fixed amount of time following the replacement of an air conditioning unit before work on the network may commence. This fixed delay is known as a:
- ○ A. Float
- ○ B. Fly-box
- ○ C. Time-box
- ○ D. Lag

40. According to the Stakeholder Salience Model, a stakeholder who exhibits Urgency and Legitimacy without Power is said to be:
- ○ A. Dependent
- ○ B. Demanding
- ○ C. Dominant
- ○ D. Dangerous

Project Management Practice Questions for CAPM & PMP Exams

41. Consider this four activity project schedule:
- **Activity-A has a duration of 1 day and is the finish-to-start predecessor of Activities B & C.**
- **Activity-B has a duration of 2 days, while Activity-C has a duration of 8 days.**
- **Activity-D is dependent upon the completion of both Activities B & C.**

Activity-C is delayed by 3 days. Which statement is true?

○ A. Activity-C may use Activity-B's float to complete the project on schedule.
○ B. Activity-B may now have additional float
○ C. Activity-B may now have less float
○ D. Activity-B may now be on the critical path

42. The project team is currently gathering requirements for a new product to be launched in the 3rd quarter. The product owner, Daniela, suggests that it may be helpful to visually illustrate how various people and organizations will interact with the product. As project manager, you agree and address it through the development of a:

○ A. Work Breakdown Structure
○ B. Focus Group
○ C. Context Diagram
○ D. Salience Model

43. Nick has come to realize there are many variables that contribute to the overall probability of an uncertain condition. Which Tool & Technique from Perform Quantitative Risk Analysis does Nick employ to perform 'what if' analysis on the various scenarios that form a probability distribution?

○ A. Monte Carlo simulation
○ B. Fortune Wheel analysis
○ C. Parimutuel simulation
○ D. Urgency analysis

44. While working with your project team to Plan Risk Responses, it is determined that while the threat cannot be removed entirely, the associated probability and impact can be reduced by taking pro-active measures. The risk response strategy being here is:

○ A. Avoid

○ B. Mitigate

○ C. Accept

○ D. Escalate

45. The delivery of key materials planned for Week-10 of your project, is now late. If the materials are not delivered by Week-13, the project completion date will be in jeopardy. The supplier has promised that these materials should arrive in 2 weeks.

What is the total float for the activity defined by the delivery of these materials?

○ A. 2 weeks

○ B. 3 weeks

○ C. 4 weeks

○ D. 5 weeks

46. After completing the project schedule, Thaddeus discovers a project team member is assigned to conflicting activities. Which Develop Schedule Tool & Technique should he use to adjust the schedule based on the resource constraints?

○ A. Resource Loading

○ B. Resource Lagging

○ C. Resource Crashing

○ D. Resource Leveling

47. After issuing a test summary report with no significant defects, an analyst performs some additional testing where a defect is discovered and you are notified. Based on the original report, you are meeting today with stakeholders to Validate Scope and obtain their acceptance of the final deliverable. You should:

○ A. Cancel the meeting and have the defect fixed before reviewing the deliverable with stakeholders.

○ B. Proceed with the meeting to obtain acceptance, without bringing up the newly found defect since the test summary report is clean.

○ C. Proceed with the meeting, pointing out the newly discovered defect so the stakeholders can decide whether to have it fixed or accept it as-is.

○ D. Bring the analyst with you to the meeting to explain why testing continued after the test summary report was issued.

48. Incentives and awards within contracts may be used to:

○ A. Align the objectives of the buyer and the seller

○ B. Decrease the risk of non-performance

○ C. Render a contract null and void

○ D. Adjust source selection criteria

49. A scatter diagram with a horizontal trend line indicates:

○ A. A positive correlation between the two variables

○ B. A negative correlation between the two variables

○ C. No correlation between the two variables

○ D. A correlation with one variable but not the other.

50. Upon Claude's reassignment to another project, you are chosen to take over as project manager. During your first week, you observe the engineers spending an inordinate amount of their time responding to ad hoc requests from project stakeholders. You perform Variance Analysis and determine the engineering activities to be already behind schedule, and if the trend continues Critical Path will be jeopardized within the next 2 weeks.

What should you do next?

○ A. Tell the engineers to ignore all ad hoc requests from stakeholders until their work is back on schedule.

○ B. Tell the stakeholders to forward all engineering requests to you for prioritization

○ C. Refer to the communications management plan, and advise both the stakeholders and the engineers of the plan and protocols established for ad hoc information requests.

○ D. Refer to the stakeholder salience model, and advise the engineers to respond to information requests only from stakeholders in positions of power.

Practice Questions Set #7

50 multiple choice questions

*PMP
Leadership, Communications, and 'Soft Skills' Questions*

Practice Question Set #7

1. You are the project manager in a multi-national organization. How can you best prevent misunderstandings due to cross-cultural differences?

○ A. Use all appropriate methods of communications and follow up in writing when communicating verbally. Remember that cultural diversity may help project teams solve unforeseen problems over the course of the project.

○ B. Keep in mind that some cultures are more developed than others. Some have strong values, while some do not. Therefore you should avoid choosing members from countries with cultures that are not similar to your own.

○ C. Since communication habits differ significantly across various cultures, communicating between people from different countries should only be limited to verbal. The use of non-verbal communications bears too many risks.

○ D. Cultural differences can prevent a project from being successful. Project teams should be fully assimilated to ensure that cultural differences do not disrupt the work.

2. Theresa is managing a team of enthusiastic beginners, and provides them with clear instructions regarding their work, exactly how the work is to be performed, and her expectations. She is utilizing which leadership style?

○ A. Directing
○ B. Coaching
○ C. Facilitating
○ D. Empowering

3. You notice that a certain aspect of the project's scope is the source of conflict between various team members who seem to only understand their assigned work but not the bigger picture. You address this by

○ A. Creating a shared understanding of project scope and deliverables

○ B. Isolating team members so that they do not interfere with other group's work

○ C. Forming virtual teams

○ D. Facilitating the team members to compromise their positions

4. One of your engineers appears to be constantly checking his phone and replying to text messages while another team member is presenting their findings. You notice this, and coach the engineer on which communication technique:
- ○ A. Feedback
- ○ B. Active Listening
- ○ C. The 5 C's of Communication
- ○ D. Noise

5. Several team members disagree on a design approach. You recognize the importance of not only a good design choice, but also consensus toward a joint decision. You encourage:
- ○ A. Compromise
- ○ B. Competence
- ○ C. Collaboration
- ○ D. Co-location

6. Empathy is a key ingredient in developing emotional intelligence. As a leader, the project manager should develop empathy through the awareness of
- ○ A. the competence of highly skilled resources
- ○ B. other people's feelings especially when making decisions
- ○ C. the impact of delays on project deliverables
- ○ D. the value of the project outcomes

7. The Leadership style that not only addresses the project objectives, but also the developmental and professional growth of the project team members is known as:
- ○ A. Servant Leadership
- ○ B. Transformational Leadership
- ○ C. Transactional Leadership
- ○ D. Situational Leadership

8. Your organization has engaged in a new relationship with consulting resources with vast industry experience. Your begin to leverage these consultants to provide expertise in specific design elements in your project, with the consultants working from their remote offices. You should immediately consider:

- A. the cost of travel and expenses
- B. optimizing the performance of the consulting team
- C. transitioning the existing project team members to new consulting roles
- D. forming the relationship between the consultants and your existing project team

9. As project manager, you may not have authority to provide monetary rewards to team members who perform above expectations, however, you should

- A. wait until project transition to acknowledge the performance of project team members
- B. provide recognition only to the whole team's combined effort, and not that of any one individual
- C. do nothing, since only monetary rewards are the only effective recognition of individual accomplishment
- D. formally recognize the efforts of the individual team members throughout the project life cycle

10. Greta is establishing a knowledge repository for her project, but is having difficulty recording this type of knowledge inherent with the more experienced members of the organization:

- A. Explicit
- B. Implicit
- C. Codified
- D. Tacit

11. The key emphasis of Servant Leadership is

- A. to manage project tasks
- B. to reward high performance
- C. to facilitate collaboration
- D. to hold team members accountable for their behaviors

12. Two of your project team members are at odds over a requirement specification for which there is no urgency to resolve. This conflict, however, is distracting and disrupting the team's work habits. The best approach for dealing with this is:

○ A. Force/Direct a decision in favor of a single resolution immediately

○ B. Withdraw/Avoid since there is time for the conflict to work its way out

○ C. Facilitate a Compromise between the two team members

○ D. Have team members vote on which approach they like best

13. Letitia appears to be withdrawn and not contributing in team discussions where she has previously shown herself to be well versed. As project manager, you should first:

○ A. Discuss the situation with her manager

○ B. Record the activity as a project risk

○ C. Solicit her input as a valued team member

○ D. Try to solve her emotional issues

14. According to the Salience Model of Stakeholder Classification, a Dormant Stakeholder:

○ A. Urgency, without Power or Legitimacy

○ B. Legitimacy, without Power or Urgency

○ C. Power, without Urgency or Legitimacy

○ D. Power and Legitimacy, without Urgency

15. Roland is managing a project where team members and stakeholders range in ages from their mid-20's through early 60's. Which of the following processes would NOT necessarily be affected by this diversity?

○ A. Control Procurements

○ B. Manage Team

○ C. Monitor Stakeholder Engagement

○ D. Plan Communications Management

16. A conflict arises between two project resources during an early stage of your project. You see this as situation that could eventually lead to bigger problems in the team's morale and ultimately effect the project's performance. You handle the conflict by:
○ A. Meeting with the two resources privately, emphasizing their areas of agreement in an attempt to smooth.
○ B. Deciding which resource has the superior approach, and announcing your decision during the next full team meeting.
○ C. Using emotional intelligence, you determine which of the two resources is less passionate about defending their stance and persuade them to back down for the good of the team.
○ D. Escalating the conflict to the project sponsor for senior management to resolve.

17. Situational Leadership teaches us that
○ A. The leader should select a style of leadership that he is most adept.
○ B. The leader should adapt his leadership style based on conditions and circumstances
○ C. The Leader should always maintain an authoritarian disposition
○ D. The Leader should fully empower the team, regardless of their capabilities

18. Erin is nearing completion of her first project, and has already been assigned to another project that will initiate next week. She is excited to start researching the scope of her new work, but understands she must hand over the deliverables of her current project to the customer. What should Erin do next?
○ A. Obtain stakeholder approval for the current project deliverable, and lead the team towards formal project closure.
○ B. Delegate responsibility of all remaining work on the current project to a business analyst, thereby freeing time get started on the new project.
○ C. Delay the initiation of the new project until all current project activities have been completed.
○ D. Close the current project immediately, providing the customer with 'as is' deliverables.

19. Which of the following is a Tool/Technique of Manage Stakeholder Engagement, categorized as Interpersonal and Team Skills:
○ A. Mind Mapping
○ B. Benchmarking
○ C. Configuration Management
○ D. Cultural Awareness

20. A project manager with highly developed skills in emotional intelligence would engage in such behaviors as
○ A. Recognizing the time when the project sponsor must intervene to direct a decision
○ B. Recognizing when to crash the project schedule
○ C. Recognizing which team members are deserving of formal acknowledgment
○ D. Recognizing when a team member needs help but is too embarrassed to ask.

21. Active Listening teaches us to :
○ A. Listen attentively, with patience and empathy
○ B. Listen aggressively, with speed and efficiency
○ C. Listen coherently, with clarity and completeness
○ D. Listen selectively, with efficiency and effectiveness

22. Sioban accepts others for what they are and openly exhibits concern for others. This personality characteristic is known as:
○ A. Managerial
○ B. Emotional
○ C. Social
○ D. Authentic

23. By changing or removing organizational impediments from becoming bottlenecks that might prevent the team from quickly delivering valuable products or services, the project manager is operating as:
○ A. Servant/Leader
○ B. Transformational Leader
○ C. Charismatic Leader
○ D. Laissez Faire Leader

24. **The CFO of your organization approved of your project budget, but generally has a low level of interest in the outcomes of your project. You apply this stakeholder management strategy:**
- ○ A. Monitor Only
- ○ B. Manage Closely
- ○ C. Keep Informed
- ○ D. Keep Satisfied

25. **Teri is managing a team of competent, yet cautious individuals. She chooses which of the following leadership style to provide guidance and support, while building their confidence in making decisions:**
- ○ A. Directing
- ○ B. Coaching
- ○ C. Facilitating
- ○ D. Empowering

26. **The entire organization is cautious around Margaret, the CEO's administrative assistant. They all understand the depth of Margaret's :**
- ○ A. Expert power
- ○ B. Legitimate power
- ○ C. Referent power
- ○ D. Representative power

27. **Which of the following is regarded as the most important aspect of Knowledge Management**
- ○ A. Ensuring thorough documentation so that knowledge can be shared.
- ○ B. Creating an atmosphere of trust, so that people are motivated to share their knowledge.
- ○ C. Obtaining lessons learned at the end of the project, in order for it to be used in future projects.
- ○ D. Emphasize codified explicit knowledge, since it is not subject to different interpretations.

28. Activities designed to enhance the skills, knowledge, and capabilities of the project team is called:
○ A. Roles and Responsibilities
○ B. Ground Rules
○ C. Reward and Recognition
○ D. Training

29. Jacinta attended a conference where she learned a valuable skill, and has begun to apply it by reducing tension and increasing cooperation among the project team members. Jacinta has likely learned this tool:
○ A. Earned Value Management
○ B. Emotional Intelligence
○ C. Management by Objectives
○ D. Situational Leadership

30. Select the statement that accurately describes a difference between Management and Leadership
○ A. Management is reliant on controls, while Leadership is built on trust
○ B. Management relies on Expert Power, while leadership relies on Formal, or Positional Power
○ C. Management is concerned with long-range vision, while Leadership is focused on short-term goals
○ D. Management will seek to innovate, while Leadership will maintain and administrate

31. Since the project manager often has little or no direct authority over team members in a matrixed environment, the project manager must influence stakeholders through the all of these key skills, EXCEPT:
○ A. Ability to be persuasive
○ B. Active Listening skills
○ C. Coersion, implicit or explicit
○ D. Awareness of, and consideration for, varying perceptions within a given situation

32. Which of the following is an example of Pull communications?
- A. Instant Messaging
- B. Retrieval of procedures from a knowledge repository
- C. An email sent to all project team members
- D. Video-conferencing

33. All of the following behaviors can build and sustain credibility with project stakeholders, EXCEPT:
- A. Being flexible and open to new ideas
- B. Being respectful
- C. Being quick to judge and unapologetic
- D. Being reliable and committed

34. You are told that one of the project analysts presented the work of a junior analyst as her own, without giving appropriate credit. What should you do next?
- A. Discuss the situation with the analyst's functional manager
- B. Report the situation to the human resources department
- C. Assess the credibility of the accusations before taking any action
- D. Do nothing since the project analysts are not under your direct authority

35. You notice that risk management is not effective, and that team members and stakeholders are often caught off guard by the unexpected. You consider conducting a
- A. Risk Audit
- B. Risk Response
- C. Quantitative Risk Analysis
- D. Monte Carlo Simulation

36. Leadership skills used to Manage Stakeholder Engagement include all, EXCEPT:
- A. Facilitate consensus towards project objectives
- B. Influence people to support the project
- C. Negotiate agreements to satisfy project needs
- D. Withhold project information to avoid resistance

37. In the Stakeholder Engagement Matrix, the level where the stakeholder is actively engaged in ensuring project success is known as:
- ○ A. Leading
- ○ B. Supporting
- ○ C. Active
- ○ D. Neutral

38. Leveraging diversity is part of Social Awareness; this includes:
- ○ A. respect for all cultures and values
- ○ B. building and expanding social networks
- ○ C. giving feedback appropriately
- ○ D. the ability to be persuasive

39. Simon is planning to hold a team meeting to discuss a recently approved change request. In planning this meeting, Simon should do all of the following, EXCEPT:
- ○ A. Prepare and distribute an agenda stating the objectives of the meeting
- ○ B. Ensure the appropriate participants are invited and attend
- ○ C. Wait to distribute agenda and any relevant information until the meeting has started.
- ○ D. Distribute any relevant information for review prior to the meeting

40. You sense that Phil has a creative personality trait, and as such will think abstractly and contribute innovative ideas that can be most valuable in which of the following project management processes:
- ○ A. Control Quality
- ○ B. Plan Risk Responses
- ○ C. Determine Budget
- ○ D. Identify Stakeholders

41. A project manager may utilize these skills to reduce tension and promote cooperation when stressful situations arise among team members:
- A. Emotional Intelligence
- B. Transactional Leadership
- C. Negotiations
- D. Networking

42. Lewis is managing a project that has experienced external delays and is now significantly behind schedule. The team is experiencing low morale due to these delays, and the anticipated pressure of being forced to make up time. Lewis should immediately:
- A. Place the project on hold so the team could be productive in other work
- B. Start planning for overtime to deliver project on schedule
- C. Boost morale through a team building event
- D. Forecast the Estimate to Completion and discuss potential changes to project baselines with the project sponsor

43. After meeting with your project sponsor and stakeholders, you discover an error in your earned value calculations that negatively impact the project status and forecast. You should:
- A. Resign in shame as human errors cannot be tolerated in field of project management
- B. Let the stakeholders know the report was incorrect, and provide them with a revised status.
- C. Wait until the next reporting cycle to correct the error.
- D. Fix the error, but do not reflect the change in the project status.

44. As project manager, you plan to conduct a Kick-off meeting at which you will discuss all of the following, EXCEPT:
- A. Project Scope, Objectives, and Known Risks
- B. Formats and frequencies for project communications
- C. Project Roles & Responsibilities
- D. Work Performance Information

45. One of your stakeholders is resistant to change and has not taken a supporting role in your project. You attempt to influence this stakeholder by:

○ A. increasing communications of project information

○ B. persuading the stakeholder through their perception of the project outcomes

○ C. compromising the level of effort required on the stakeholder's part

○ D. coercion in either implicit or explicit means

46. By making your communications coherent, your ideas are presented

○ A. with proper spelling and punctuation

○ B. logically, well connected and relevant

○ C. at the appropriate level of the audience

○ D. without necessarily agreement or understanding

47. Alison is managing a project with a team of experienced professionals who are highly competent in their job skills, but lack the motivation needed to perform to their highest potential. Alison recognizes this and uses this leadership style:

○ A. Authoritarian, or Directing style to ensure work is done accurately and to meet expectations

○ B. Coaching style, to build confidence in the team's ability to make decisions

○ C. Supporting, or Facilitating style to participate with the team in building an optimized environment

○ D. Empowering, to allow the team to self-organize and be accountable for their outcomes.

48. If a specific team resource is not pre-assigned in your project charter, you may have to negotiate the acquisition with the functional manager. All of the following criteria should be considered in the negotiation, EXCEPT:

○ A. Availability

○ B. Age

○ C. Attitude

○ D. Ability

49. All of the following are characteristics and traits of effective leaders, EXCEPT:

○ A. Confidence in believing they can handle anything
○ B. Sensitivity to other cultures, including values and beliefs
○ C. Being trustworthy and of strong character
○ D. Creativity and the capacity for abstract thought

50. In working with a functional manager, who is juggling conflicting priorities among his staff, you may have to utilize this skill to achieve a mutually acceptable agreement relative to your project's work assignments.

○ A. Transparency
○ B. Authenticity
○ C. Disruption
○ D. Negotiation

Practice Questions Set #8

50 multiple choice questions

PMP
Questions for Agile/Adaptive Life Cycles

Practice Question Set #8

1. An Agile life cycle can be used to mitigate the impact of a risk by:
- A. Avoiding technical threats through work-arounds
- B. Using frequent delivery in small increments to inspect work often and change what to do next without the high cost of rework and scrap.
- C. Conforming to the static written specification from project start to finish
- D. Bundling all of the work into a single delivery

2. What are the major properties of a cross-functional Agile team?
- A. The team is able to commit to the completion of the project deliverables within the schedule and cost baselines.
- B. The team has all the required skills needed to collectively accept ownership of completing the next increment.
- C. Each team member has all the knowledge and experience needed to achieve the project objectives.
- D. The team is comprised of specialized individuals dedicated to particular activities, who work independently to minimize interaction and maximize overall product value.

3. Which of the following is NOT an Agile tool for empirical and value-based measurements of project results
- A. Kanban Board
- B. Burn Down Chart
- C. Burn Up Chart
- D. Monte Carlo Simulation

4. It is a common practice for projects in an Agile environment to have a Daily Standup meeting. What is the purpose of this meeting?
- A. To provide status reporting on a daily basis.
- B. To solve problems as soon as they become apparent.
- C. To engage the project sponsor and stakeholders in decision making and commitment towards project objectives.
- D. To commit to near-term goals, uncover problems, and ensure that work flows smoothly through the team.

5. Which of the following is NOT a goal of a Retrospective?
  ○   A. Refinement of Backlog items in preparation for the next increment
  ○   B. Discuss impediments raised by the team during the last increment, and possible solutions than can be implemented in the next increment.
  ○   C. Discuss team interactions and how the team can improve collaboration.
  ○   D. Review and modify the definition of done, if needed.

6. Agile approaches emphasize Servant Leadership to empower
  ○   A. the team
  ○   B. the project manager
  ○   C. the stakeholders
  ○   D. the product owner

7. What would a horizontal trend line on a Burndown Chart signify?
  ○   A. No change in team capacity
  ○   B. No change in project costs
  ○   C. No change in completed work packages
  ○   D. No correlation between the two variables

8. Which of the following statements regarding 'change' is true within the Agile project environment?
  ○   A. Changes are encouraged early in the life cycle, and discouraged as the increment matures.
  ○   B. Changing requirements are welcome at any point in the agile life cycle, even in late stages of development.
  ○   C. Changes in business priorities have no impact on the Agile project's work in progress.
  ○   D. Changes to an iteration's goal is encouraged during the development of the increment.

9. The burn down chart indicates all work selected for the increment is at risk of not completing within the time-box. Your next move should be to:

○ A. Meet with the product owner and development team to determine what work can be completed within the time box, without compromising quality standards

○ B. Meet with the product owner and development team to review the status of the increment and extend the time-box accordingly.

○ C. Meet with the product owner and development team to instruct them on how they can cut corners to complete the remaining work within the time-box

○ D. Meet with the product owner and development team to cancel the current iteration, and plan a new one that will consider the team's proven capabilities in determining the length of the new iteration's time-box to deliver all backlog items.

10. Pavel is a project manager working in a fast-paced consumer electronics company. The key objectives of the project are constrained by a fixed deadline, one in which the product's market launch must coincide with the Holiday season. To maximize the value of the product's features within the given timeframe, Pavel decides to utilize:

○ A. Fast Track Life Cycle
○ B. Agile Life Cycle
○ C. Predictive Life Cycle
○ D. Critical Path Life Cycle

11. Agile life cycles work well for projects that have a high degree of

○ A. Complexity and Competence
○ B. Dependencies and Constraints
○ C. Uncertainty and Complexity
○ D. Clarity and Certainty

12. Adaptive Life Cycles, also known as Agile, utilize a concept of time-boxing to define:
- A. a minimum time for the completion of an increment
- B. a maximum time for completion of all requirements
- C. a specified period of time for the completion of an increment
- D. a variable period of time for the completion of an increment

13. Jenna is managing a project with well-defined project plan, and a complete schedule that spans from initiation through project delivery. She manages the development work according to this plan in a
- A. Predictive Life Cycle
- B. Controlling Life Cycle
- C. Incremental Life Cycle
- D. Adaptive Life Cycle

14. A project where the hardware components follow a predictive life cycle, and software development follows an agile approach is said to be managed using a
- A. Plan Driven Life Cycle
- B. Change Driven Life Cycle
- C. Hybrid Life Cycle
- D. Transitional Life Cycle

15. This tool is useful in visualizing workflow and is know as a _____ Board.
- A. Kaizen
- B. Kano
- C. Kali
- D. Kanban

16. In an Agile/Adaptive project environment, which of the following tools would be used to track work completed in the iteration?
- A. Burn-up Chart
- B. Gantt Chart
- C. Product Backlog
- D. Milestone Schedule

17. During an iteration, a team member realizes one of the backlog items selected will require more effort than originally estimated. They should

○ A. Do Nothing, backlog items cannot be changed during an iteration

○ B. Remove it from the backlog

○ C. Update the backlog item to reflect the correct estimate

○ D. Cancel the Sprint

18. Which of the following is a key success factor for Project Communications Management in an Agile/Adaptive environment?

○ A. Utilize a Virtual team whenever possible

○ B. Transparency

○ C. Infrequent stakeholder reviews

○ D. Discourage changes to project scope

19. What would a diagonal trend line that rises above the plan line signify on a Burndown Chart?

○ A. Less work is being completed than forecasted

○ B. More work is being completed than forecasted

○ C. More resources are being used to get work done

○ D. Fewer resources are being used to get work done

20. Scaling Agile, through frameworks and approaches such as Scaled Agile Framework (SAFe), Large Scaled Scrum (LSS), and Scrum of Scrums (SoS) is used to

○ A. Migrate Agile teams to function in larger, more predictive life cycles

○ B. Provide guidance for initiatives that require the collaboration of multiple Agile team

○ C. Improve the accountability of the Agile team and its leadership

○ D. Allow the Agile team to grow in size, yet retain the transparency, collaboration, and efficiency of the smaller Agile team

21. By changing or removing organizational impediments from becoming bottlenecks that might prevent the team from quickly delivering valuable products or services, the project manager is operating as a

○ A. Servant Leader

○ B. Transformational Leader

○ C. Transactional Leader

○ D. Situational Leader

22. A Retrospective in an Agile project environment is best described as

○ A. The team estimates what they can complete for the upcoming iteration.

○ B. At the conclusion of each iteration, or sprint, the project team will demonstrate the completed work for stakeholder acceptance.

○ C. The team meets daily, for 15 minutes, to identify impediments and ensure work flows smoothly through the team.

○ D. At regular intervals, the team reflects on how to become more effective then adjusts its behaviors accordingly.

23. Kanban differs from Scrum in that

○ A. Kanban is centered around time-boxed project increments, where Scrum is a continuous 'just in time' system where the next work item is pulled from an organized list of tasks .

○ B. Kanban is more closely related to a predictive life cycle, as it is change averse, while Scrum is change driven.

○ C. Kanban was conceived in Lean manufacturing's "Just in Time" process for continuous delivery, while Scrum is an Agile framework developed to deliver incremental value in a series of sprints.

○ D. Kanban is of value only in manufacturing environments, while Scrum is of value only in software development projects.

24. When working in an Agile project environment, there is an inherent need to communicate evolving and emerging details more frequently and quickly. To ensure accessibility to project artifacts and information, the project manager must promote a communication policy of:
○ A. Transparency
○ B. Empiricism
○ C. Confidentiality
○ D. Determinism

25. Adrian is managing the rollout of a new Point of Sale (POS) system to the company's 18 store locations. Since the work for each location will be similar, Adrian conforms to this type of project life cycle
○ A. Presumptive
○ B. Iterative
○ C. Predictive
○ D. Adaptive

26. In the context of an Agile Life Cycle, the Product Backlog refers to:
○ A. The time it will take for all necessary resources to arrive on the job site.
○ B. The number of days the iteration needs in order to complete the work
○ C. The collection of requirements to be estimated, prioritized and selected for inclusion for an iteration.
○ D. The current market demand for your project's deliverables.

27. The Agile team and stakeholders inspect the increment and figure out what to do next during which Agile event?
○ A. Standup Meeting
○ B. Retrospective
○ C. Release planning
○ D. Review

28. Which of the following is the primary objective of Planning for Iteration-based Agile

○ A. Reviewing current functionality that supports the new solution

○ B. Updating the product scope with all milestone end dates and cost estimates

○ C. Recalculating velocity, adjusting team capacity, and forecasting the project delivery date

○ D. Understanding what functionality is chosen for the next iteration and figuring out how to do it.

29. Which of the following is NOT a part of Product Backlog Refinement?

○ A. Reviewing completed Product Backlog items with the stakeholders

○ B. Decomposition of the Product Backlog

○ C. Clarifying and adding detail to a Product Backlog item

○ D. Adding estimates to the Product Backlog items

30. In tracking team performance, you notice a negative variance to plan due to unexpected absences and delays in the completion of dependencies from external sources. You recommend:

○ A. Allocating a higher percentage of time for unplanned activities in future iterations

○ B. Augmenting the Agile team to remove dependencies on all external sources

○ C. Shorten the estimates of the activities within the Agile team's control

○ D. Lengthen the duration of the future iterations

31. Cadence refers to the

○ A. Team's rhythm of execution in terms of a development cycle

○ B. Performance of an individual, or group of individuals

○ C. Number of combined team hours available for work in an iteration

○ D. Amount of work in hours or 'story points' the team can complete in an iteration

32. The project sponsor would like to understand the team's performance during the last iteration. Which of the following would be appropriate for you to review with the sponsor?
- ○ A. Product Backlog
- ○ B. Pareto Chart
- ○ C. Velocity Chart
- ○ D. Sprint Backlog

33. In the daily standup meeting, it is discussed how test data must be created to demonstrate the increment's functionality. In order to ensure all test data is ready for the iteration's review, you recommend:
- ○ A. canceling the demonstration/review
- ○ B. preparing a Pareto chart and checksheet
- ○ C. submitting a change request for authorization
- ○ D. creating a user story to prepare the appropriate test data

34. Transparency is a key enabler in a Lean environment because
- ○ A. Transparency allows all team members an equal voice
- ○ B. Transparency makes waste visible so that it can be removed
- ○ C. Transparency protects the organization from legal action
- ○ D. Transparency reduces the need for collaboration

35. A team member is removed from the Agile team by his functional manager to work on a new high-priority assignment on another project. As a result, the team will not be able complete all the user stories selected for the increment. You should
- ○ A. Cancel the iteration
- ○ B. Lengthen the duration of the iteration
- ○ C. Meet with the sponsor and stakeholders to re-examine expectations for the increment
- ○ D. Postpone the work assigned to the removed team member to the next iteration

Project Management Practice Questions for CAPM & PMP Exams

36. Which of the following statements may lead the organization's management to view the Agile process negatively?

○ A. Stakeholders are engaged in product inspections less frequently

○ B. Decomposing work into incremental deliverables may involve some rework

○ C. Self-organizing teams tend to be less collaborative

○ D. Agile takes controls away from the organization's management

37. Lean Software Development uses this tool to identify and eliminate waste

○ A. Value Stream Mapping

○ B. Kanban Board

○ C. Burndown Charts

○ D. Decomposition

38. Which of the following does the Agile team do during the first iteration?

○ A. Develop and deliver at least one piece of functionality in a releasable increment

○ B. Develop a plan for the rest of the project

○ C. Determine the complete architecture and infrastructure for the product

○ D. Create the complete Product Backlog that will be developed in subsequent iterations

39. Extreme Programming (XP) is an Agile software development method that promotes high-quality software through all of the following, EXCEPT:

○ A. Listening to the customer to determine their needs

○ B. Error-free code to eliminate the need for testing

○ C. Maintaining a sustainable pace for development Deployments

○ D. Continuous integration and incremental deployments

40. Which of the following is NOT a goal of the Retrospective?

○ A. Discuss impediments raised by the team during the last increment, and possible solutions than can be implemented in the next.
○ B. Refinement of Product Backlog items in preparation for the next increment.
○ C. Discuss team interactions and how the team can improve collaboration.
○ D. Review, modify, and/or clarify the 'Definition of Done'.

41. A team member, Carla, is expected to divide her time equally between your project and another project. Which of the following would most likely occur as a result of Carla's dual assigments?

○ A. Work that is only partially completed
○ B. An increase in defects due to carelessness
○ C. A decrease in performance due to task switching
○ D. An increase in overall performance

42. During which Agile event is the increment determined to be released

○ A. Planning
○ B. Daily Standup
○ C. Review
○ D. Retrospective

43. A member of the Agile team is delayed due to an unanswered request for clarification of a requirement specification from a project stakeholder. Which of the following describes the best course of action:

○ A. The Servant Leader reaches out to the stakeholder on behalf of the team member
○ B. The stakeholder is invited to the Retrospective to better understand the team's needs
○ C. The duration of the iteration is extended to account for the loss of time
○ D. The issue is reflected in the Burndown chart

44. After the product owner presents the team with a prioritized list of features ordered by business value, the team should begin:

○ A. Estimating the effort

○ B. Developing the code

○ C. Acquiring resources

○ D. Decomposing the features into user stories

45. Which statement is true regarding documentation in an Agile environment?

○ A. There is no documentation in the Agile projects

○ B. Documentation is replaced by transparency in Agile projects

○ C. Documentation is done only after all project work is completed and accepted by the customer

○ D. Documentation is secondary to working solutions

46. In the Servant Leader role, the project manager is most likely to

○ A. Determine cost and schedule variances

○ B. Prioritize the backlog items

○ C. Resolve issues encountered by the Agile team

○ D. Demonstrate the increment's features to project stakeholders

47. In what order is work prioritized in the product backlog, while considering dependencies and risks?

○ A. by complexity, as determined by the development team

○ B. by value, as determined by the product owner

○ C. by a vote, as facilitated by the project manager

○ D. by receipt, first in / first out

48. A project is being planned to construct and install an outdoor storage unit. The steps are very predictable, and does not appear to have any significant risks. The life cycle selected as suitable for this project would be

○ A. Adaptive
○ B. Predictive
○ C. Iterative
○ D. Incremental

49. A person who can train, mentor, and guide organizations and teams through the transformation to an Agile environment is known as:

○ A. Servant Leader
○ B. Project Sponsor
○ C. Project Owner
○ D. Agile Coach

50. A User Story is tool used in Agile software development

○ A. to define the length of the team's development cycle, from start to finish, needed to create a potentially releasable increment.

○ B. to capture the description of a software feature from an end-user perspective, describing the type of user, what they want, and why.

○ C. to visualize work, limit work-in-progress, and maximize efficiency and flow.

○ D. to summarize the vision and direction of a product offering over time.

ONLINE:

Link to Interactive Tests

- Question Set #1
- Question Set #2
- Question Set #3
- Question Set #4
- ➢ CAPM 150 Question Practice Test
- Question Set #5
- Question Set #6
- Question Set #7
- Question Set #8
- ➢ PMP 200 Question Practice Test

PLUS...
- ITTO Challenge!
- ITTO Flow!
- Critical Path Challenge!
- What Comes Next?
- And more study tools to come...

https://testmoz.com/class/18629

Type the above link into the address bar of your browser to access the menu.

ANSWERS

Practice Question Set #1 - ANSWERS

1. D

PMBOK Chapter 1 Introduction, Section 1.2 Foundational Elements

2. B

PMBOK Chapter 3 The Role of the Project Manager, Section 3.4 Project Manager Competences

3. C

PMBOK Chapter 1 Introduction, Section 1.2 Foundational Elements

4. B

PMBOK Chapter 1 Introduction, Section 1.2 Foundational Elements

5. B

PMBOK Chapter 1 Introduction, Section 1.2.4.1 Project and Development Life Cycles

6. D

PMBOK Part 2 The Standard for Project Management, Section 1.5 The Project Life Cycle (fig 1-3 Impact of Variables Over Time)

7. A

PMBOK Chapter 1 Introduction, Section 1.2.4.1 Project and Development Life Cycles

8. A

PMBOK Chapter 1 Introduction, Section 1.2.4.5 Project Management Process Groups

9. 5
    <u>1</u>
    3
    <u>2</u>
    4

PMBOK Part 2: The Standard for Project Management, Section 1.9 (Table 1.1 Project Management Process Group and Knowledge Area Mapping)

10. B

PMBOK Chapter 1 Introduction, Section 1.2.4.5 Project Management Process Groups

PMBOK Chapter 8 Quality, Section 8.1 Plan Quality Management

11. D

PMBOK Chapter 1 Introduction, Section 1.2.4.1 Project and Development Life Cycles

12. A, B, D

PMBOK Chapter 4 Project Integration Management, Section 4.1 Develop Project Charter

13. A

PMBOK Chapter 4 Project Integration Management, fig 4.1 Overview

14. A

PMBOK Chapter 4 Project Integration Management, Section 4.6 Perform Integrated Change Control

15. C

PMBOK Chapter 4 Project Integration Management, Section 4.6 Perform Integrated Change Control

16. D

PMBOK Chapter 5 Project Scope Management, Section 5.1.3 Plan Scope Management : Outputs

17. D

PMBOK Chapter 5 Project Scope Management, Section 5.2.1 Collect Requirements : Inputs

18. A

PMBOK Chapter 5 Project Scope Management, Section 5.4.3 Create WBS : Outputs

19. A

PMBOK Chapter 5 Project Scope Management, Section 5.5 Validate Scope

Project Management Practice Questions for CAPM & PMP Exams

20. B

PMBOK Chapter 6 Project Schedule Management, Section 6.2.3 Define Activities : Outputs

21. A

PMBOK Chapter 6 Project Schedule Management, Trends and Emerging Practices in Project Schedule Management

22. B

PMBOK Chapter 6 Project Schedule Management, Section 6.4.2 Estimate Activity Durations : Tools and Techniques

23. B

PMBOK Chapter 6 Project Schedule Management, Section 6.5.2 Develop Schedule : Tools and Techniques (Critical Path Method)

Questions #24 & #25 reference this project schedule:

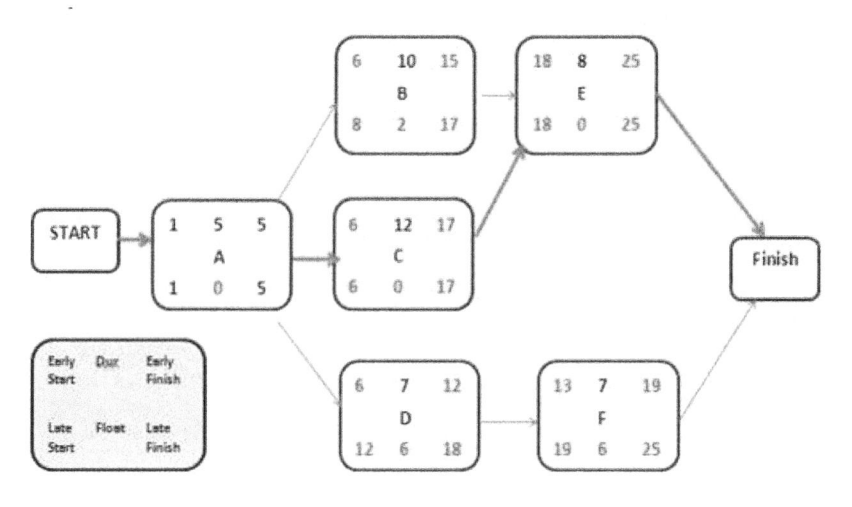

24. B

PMBOK Chapter 6 Project Schedule Management, Section 6.5.2 Develop Schedule :Tools and Techniques (Critical Path Method)

Determine the Critical Path by doing the 'forward pass' to calculate early start and early finish dates. The critical path will have the greatest duration from project start to finish.

* Answer B, Path A-C-E is correct having a total duration of 25

25. C

PMBOK Chapter 6 Project Schedule Management, Section 6.5.2 Develop Schedule :Tools and Techniques (Critical Path Method)

Determine the Total Float by doing the 'backward pass' to calculate late start and late finish dates. The Total Float is calculated by subtracting the early finish date from the late finish date. All activities on a non critical path will have the same Total Float, while all activities on the critical path will have zero Total Float.

* Answer C, Path A-D-F is correct having a total float of 6.

26. C, E

PMBOK Chapter 6 Project Schedule Management, Section 6.5.2 Develop Schedule : Tools and Techniques (Schedule Compression)

27. C

PMBOK Chapter 6 Project Schedule Management, Section 6.5.2 Develop Schedule : Tools and Techniques (Schedule Compression)

28. B

PMBOK Chapter 7 Project Cost Management

29. A, B, D

PMBOK Chapter 6 Project Schedule Management, Section 6.4.2 Estimate Activity Durations : Tools and Techniques

30. B

PMBOK Chapter 7 Project Cost Management, Section 7.4.2 Control Costs : Tools and Techniques (Variance Analysis)

31. C

PMBOK Chapter 7 Project Cost Management, Section 7.4.2 Control Costs : Tools and Techniques (Forecasting)

* The assumption states 'all future work will be accomplished at the budgeted rate', so we use the formula EAC = AC + (BAC-EV)

* Therefore, Answer C is correct. 120 + (200-80) = 240

32. D

PMBOK Chapter 7 Project Cost Management, Section 7.4.2 Control Costs : Tools and Techniques (Variance Analysis)

Project Management Practice Questions for CAPM & PMP Exams

33. D
PMBOK Chapter 7 Project Cost Management, Section 7.4.2 Control Costs : Tools and Techniques (Variance Analysis)

34. C
PMBOK Chapter 8 Project Quality Management, Key Concepts for Project Quality Management

35. A, B, C, D
PMBOK Chapter 8 Project Quality Management, Section 8.1 Plan Quality Management (fig 8.5 Cost of Quality)

36. B
PMBOK Chapter 8 Project Quality Management, Section 8.2 Manage Quality

37. A
PMBOK Chapter 8 Project Quality Management, Section 8.3.2 Control Quality : Tools and Techniques (Data Representation / Control Charts)

38. D
PMBOK Chapter 9 Project Resource Management, Section 9.1 Plan Resource Management

39. A, C, D, E, G
PMBOK Chapter 9 Project Resource Management, Section 9.5.2 Manage Team : Tools and Techniques (Interpersonal and Team Skills / Conflict Management)

40.
1. __1__
2. __2__
3. 3
4. 4

PMBOK Chapter 9 Project Resource Management, Section 9.1.2 Plan Resource Management : Tools and Techniques (Data Representation / Assignment Matrix)

41. C
PMBOK Chapter 10 Project Communications Management, Section 10.1.2 Plan Communications Management : Tools and Techniques (Communications Methods)

42. B
PMBOK Chapter 10 Project Communications Management, Section 10.1.2.4 Plan Communications Management : Tools and Techniques (Communications Models)

43. A
PMBOK Chapter 10 Project Communications Management
* Communications Channels = n (n - 1) / 2, where n= # of stakeholders
* Answer A is correct since 12 (12 - 1) / 2 = 66

44. B
PMBOK Chapter 11 Project Risk Management, Key Concepts for Project Risk Management

45. A
PMBOK Chapter 11 Project Risk Management, Section 11.2.3 Identify Risks : Outputs

46. 3
    <u>2</u>
    <u>1</u>
PMBOK Chapter 11 Project Risk Management, Section 11.5.2 Plan Risk Responses: Tools and Techniques (Strategies for Threats, Strategies for Opportunities)

47. C
PMBOK Chapter 12 Project Procurement Management, Section 12.1.3 Plan Procurement Management : Outputs (Bid Documents)

48. B
PMBOK Chapter 12 Project Procurement Management, Section 12.1.1.Plan Procurement Management : Inputs (Organizations Process Assets / Contract Types)

49. B
PMBOK Chapter 12 Project Procurement Management, Key Concepts for Project Procurement Management

50. C
PMBOK Chapter 13 Project Stakeholder Management, Section 13.1 Identify Stakeholders

Practice Question Set #2 - ANSWERS

1. A
PMBOK Chapter 3 The Role of the Project Manager, Section 3.2 Definition of a Project Manager

2. A, D, E
PMBOK Chapter 3 The Role of the Project Manager, Section 3.2 Definition of a Project Manager

3. D
PMBOK Chapter 1 Introduction, Section 1.2.3 Relationship of Project, Program, Portfolio, and Operations Management

4. B
PMBOK Chapter 1 Introduction, Section 1.2.4.3 Phase Gate

5. B
PMBOK Part 2 The Standard for Project Management, Section 1.5 The Project Life Cycle

6. D
PMBOK Chapter 1 Introduction, Section 1.2.4.5 Project Management Process Groups

7. B
PMBOK Chapter 1 Introduction, Section 1.2.4.5 Project Management Process Groups
PMBOK Chapter 4 Project Integration Management, Section 4.7 Close Project or Phase

8. B
PMBOK Chapter 4 Project Integration Management, Section 4.1.1 Develop Project Charter : Inputs

9. A
PMBOK Chapter 2 The Environment in which Projects Operate, Section 2.3 Organizational Process Assets
PMBOK Chapter 4 Project Integration Management, Section 4.2.1 Develop Project Management Plan : Inputs

10. D
PMBOK Chapter 4 Project Integration Management, Section 4.3 Direct and Manage Project Work
* note: the question refers to implementation of an <u>approved</u> change request.

11. A, B, D
PMBOK Chapter 4 Project Integration Management, Section 4.3.3 Direct and Manage Project Work : Outputs

12. A
PMBOK Chapter 4 Project Integration Management, Section 4.2.3 Develop Project Management Plan Outputs : Baselines
PMBOK Chapter 5 Project Scope Management, Section 5.4.3 Create WBS Outputs : Scope Baseline

13. C
PMBOK Chapter 5 Project Scope Management, Section 5.3.3 Define Scope Outputs : Project Scope Statement

14. A, B, D
PMBOK Chapter 5 Project Scope Management, Section 5.2.2 Collect Requirements : Tools and Techniques

15. D
PMBOK Chapter 5 Project Scope Management, Section 5.4 Create WBS

16. A
PMBOK Chapter 6 Project Schedule Management, Section 6.3.2 Sequence Activities : Tools and Techniques (Precedence Diagramming Method)
PMBOK Chapter 6 Project Schedule Management, fig 6.10 Examples of Leads and Lags

17. 3
   <u>4</u>
     <u>2</u>
       <u>1</u>

PMBOK Chapter 6 Project Schedule Management, Section 6.3.2 Sequence Activities : Tools and Techniques (Precedence Diagramming Method)

18. C
PMBOK Chapter 6 Project Schedule Management, Section 6.3.2 Sequence Activities : Tools and Techniques (Dependency Determination and Integration)

19. B
PMBOK Chapter 6 Project Schedule Management, Section 6.4.2 Estimate Activity Durations : Tools and Techniques

Project Management Practice Questions for CAPM & PMP Exams

20. C
PMBOK Chapter 5 Project Scope Management, Key Concepts for Project Scope Management & Considerations for Agile/Adaptive Environments
PMBOK Chapter 6 Project Schedule Management, Section 6.4.2 Estimate Activity Durations : Tools and Techniques (Meetings)

21. D
PMBOK Chapter 7 Project Cost Management, Section 7.2.2 Estimate Costs : Tools and Techniques

22. A
PMBOK Chapter 7 Project Cost Management, Section 7.4.2 Control Costs : Tools and Techniques
  Planned Value (PV) = $6,000
  Earned Value (EV) = $20,000 * 25% = $5,000
  Schedule Variance (SV) = EV - PV
  Schedule Variance (SV) = 5,000 - 6,000 = (-1,000)
  a Schedule Variance that is less than zero denotes a status of behind schedule.

23. A
PMBOK Chapter 7 Project Cost Management, Section 7.4.3 Control Costs : Outputs

24. C
PMBOK Chapter 7 Project Cost Management, Section 7.4.2 Control Costs : Tools and Techniques (Variance Analysis)
  Cost Variance (CV) = EV - AC
  Cost Variance (CV) = $14,000 - $12,000 = $2,000

25. <u>2</u>
  <u>7</u>
  <u>6</u>
  <u>4</u>
  <u>3</u>
  <u>1</u>
  5
PMBOK Chapter 8 Project Quality Management, Section 8.3 Control Quality

26. A
PMBOK Chapter 8 Project Quality Management, Key Concepts for Project Quality Management

27. C
PMBOK Chapter 8 Project Quality Management, Section 8.1.2 Plan Quality Management : Tools and Techniques (fig. 8.5 Cost of Quality)

28. B
PMBOK Chapter 9 Project Resource Management, Section 9.1.2 Plan Resource Management : Tools and Techniques (Hierarchical Charts)
PMBOK Chapter 9 Project Resource Management, Section 9.2.3 Estimate Activity Resources : Outputs (fig. 9.7 Sample Resource Breakdown Structure)

29. A
PMBOK Chapter 9 Project Resource Management, Trends and Emerging Practices in Project Resource Management (Virtual Teams/Distributed Teams)

30. 3
    5
    1
    4
    2
PMBOK Chapter 9 Project Resource Management, Section 9.4 Develop Team

31. D
PMBOK Chapter 10 Project Communications Management, Section 10.2.2 Plan Communications Management : Tools and Techniques (Communication Methods)

32. A
PMBOK Chapter 10 Project Communications Management, Section 10.2.2 Plan Communications Management : Tools and Techniques (Communication Models)

33. B
PMBOK Chapter 10 Project Communications Management, Section 10.2.2 Plan Communications Management : Tools and Techniques (Communication Models)

34. C
PMBOK Chapter 10 Project Communications Management, Section 10.2.2 Plan Communications Management : Tools and Techniques (Communication Models)

Project Management Practice Questions for CAPM & PMP Exams

35. C
PMBOK Chapter 11 Project Risk Management, Key Concepts for Project Risk Management

36. B, C, F
PMBOK Chapter 11 Project Risk Management, Section 11.3.2 Perform Qualitative Risk Analysis : Tools and Techniques

37. B
PMBOK Chapter 11 Project Risk Management, Section 11.3.2 Perform Qualitative Risk Management : Tools and Techniques
    R1 = $1000 * 40% = $400
    R2 = $2000 * 30% = $600
    R3 = $5000 * 10% = $500
    R4 = $800 * 50% = $400
    Total EMV = 400+600+500+400 = $1,900

38. C
PMBOK Chapter 11 Project Risk Management, Section 11.5.2 Plan Risk Responses : Tools and Techniques (Strategies for Threats)

39. D
PMBOK Chapter 11 Project Risk Management, Section 11.5.1 Plan Risk Responses : Inputs

40. C
PMBOK Chapter 12 Project Procurement Management, Section 12.1.3 Plan Procurement Management : Outputs

41. A
PMBOK Chapter 12 Project Procurement Management, Section 12.1.1 Plan Procurement Management : Inputs (Organizational Process Assets / Contract Types)

42. A
PMBOK Chapter 12 Project Procurement Management, Section 12.1.3 Plan Procurement Management : Outputs (Procurement Documents)

43. B
PMBOK Chapter 12 Project Procurement Management, Section 12.2.2 Conduct Procurements: Tools and Techniques (Interpersonal and Team Skills)

44. B
PMBOK Chapter 13 Project Stakeholder Management, Section 13.1 Identify Stakeholders

45. D
PMBOK Chapter 13 Project Stakeholder Management, Section 13.3.2 Manage Stakeholder Engagement : Tools and Techniques (Interpersonal and Team Skills)

46. C
PMBOK Chapter 13 Project Stakeholder Management, Section 13.2 Plan Stakeholder Engagement

47. A
PMBOK Chapter 13 Project Stakeholder Management, Section 13.2.2 Plan Stakeholder Engagement : Tools and Techniques (Data Representation / Stakeholder Engagement Assessment Matrix)

48. A
PMBOK Chapter 13 Project Stakeholder Management, Section 13.1.3 Identify Stakeholders : Outputs

49. B
PMBOK Chapter 2 The Environment in which Projects Operate, Section 2.2 Enterprise Environmental Factors

50. C
PMBOK Chapter 4 Project Integration Management, Section 4.2.1 Develop Project Management Plan

Project Management Practice Questions for CAPM & PMP Exams

Practice Question Set #3 - ANSWERS

1. A

PMBOK Chapter 1 Introduction, Section 1.2.4.1 Project and Development Life Cycles

2. A

PMBOK Chapter 1 Introduction, Section 1.2 Foundational Elements

3. C, D

PMBOK Chapter 2 The Environment in which Projects Operate

4. <u>1</u>
<u>3</u>
<u>2</u>
<u>5</u>
<u>4</u>

PMBOK Chapter 3 The Role of the Project Manager, Section 3.4 Project Manager Competencies : Politics, Power, and Getting Things Done

5. B

PMBOK Glossary, Section 3 Definitions

6. A, B, D

PMBOK Chapter 3 The Role of the Project Manager, Section 3.4 Project Manager Competencies

7. C

PMBOK Part 2 The Standard for Project Management, Section 4 The Executing Process Group

8. A

PMBOK Chapter 2 The Environment in which Projects Operate, Section 2.2 Enterprise Environmental Factors

9. A

PMBOK Chapter 1 Introduction, Section 1.2.6 Project Business Documents

10. A, B, C

PMBOK Chapter 4 Project Integration Management, Section 4.2 Develop Project Management Plan

11. D

PMBOK Chapter 4 Project Integration Management, Section 4.2.1 Develop Project Management Plan : Inputs

12. B

PMBOK Chapter 5 Project Scope Management, Section 5.2.3 Collect Requirements: Outputs (Requirements Traceability Matrix)

13. C

PMBOK Chapter 4 Project Integration Management, Section 4.6.2 Perform Integrated Change Control : Tools and Techniques (Change Control Tools)

14. A

PMBOK Chapter 5 Project Scope Management, Section 5.4.2.2 Create WBS : Tools and Techniques (Decomposition)

15. D

PMBOK Chapter 5 Project Scope Management, Section 5.6 Control Scope

16. B

PMBOK Chapter 5 Project Scope Management, Section 5.3.3 Define Scope : Outputs (Project Scope Statement)

17. A

PMBOK Chapter 5 Project Scope Management, Section 5.4.2.2 Create WBS : Tools and Techniques (Decomposition)

18. A

PMBOK Chapter 5 Project Scope Management, Section 5.5.2 Validate Scope : Tools and Techniques

19. A

PMBOK Chapter 5 Project Scope Management, Section 5.5.2 Validate Scope

20. C

PMBOK Chapter 6 Project Schedule Management, Section 6.3.2 Sequence Activities : Tools and Techniques (Precedence Diagramming Method)

Project Management Practice Questions for CAPM & PMP Exams

21. B

PMBOK Chapter 6 Project Schedule Management, Section 6.4.2 Estimate Activity Durations : Tools and Techniques Validate Scope

Questions #22 - #24 reference this project schedule:

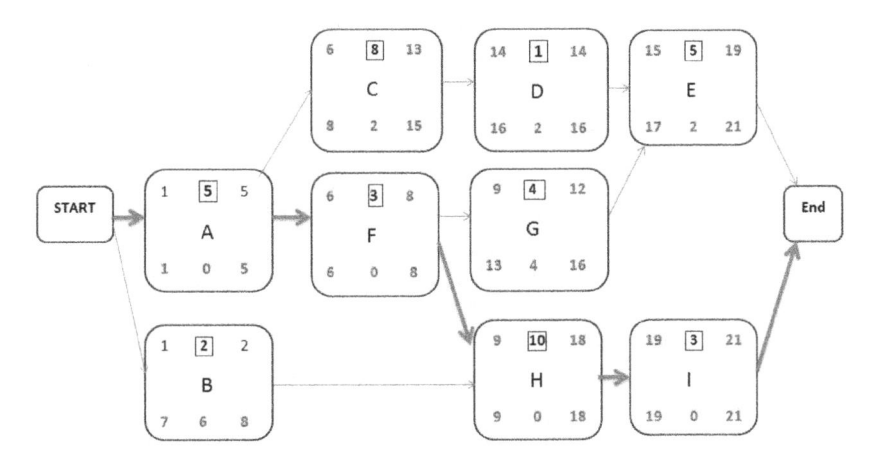

22. B

PMBOK Chapter 6 Project Schedule Management, Section 6.5.2 Develop Schedule : Tools and Techniques (Critical Path Method)

Determine the Total Float by first doing the 'forward pass' to calculate early start and early finish dates, then by doing the 'backward pass' to calculate late start and late finish dates. The total float is equal to the late finish minus early finish.

Activities A, F, H, and I are on the critical path, therefore have no float

Activity B has 6 days float, <u>making B. the correct answer</u>

Activity C and D have 2 days float

Activity G (not provided as a multiple choice) has 4 days float

142

23. D
PMBOK Chapter 6 Project Schedule Management, Section 6.5.2 Develop Schedule : Tools and Techniques (Critical Path Method)

Determine the Critical Path by doing the 'forward pass.' Activities A, F, H, and I make up the critical path The total duration of these four activities = 5+3+10+3 = 21

24. D
PMBOK Chapter 6 Project Schedule Management, Section 6.5.2 Develop Schedule : Tools and Techniques (Critical Path Method)

Determine the Total Float by first doing the 'forward pass' to calculate early start and early finish dates, then by doing the 'backward pass' to calculate late start and late finish dates. The total float is equal to the late finish minus early finish.

Activities A, F, H, and I make up the critical path

Activity C, D, and E have 2 days total float

The total float is shared between all activities on a non-critical path. Therefore, when Activities C and D each use a day of the total float, it leaves Activity E with zero (0) days float.

25. A
PMBOK Chapter 6 Project Schedule Management, Section 6.5.2 Develop Schedule : Tools and Techniques (Schedule Compression)

26. B
PMBOK Chapter 6 Project Schedule Management, Section 6.3.2 Sequence Activities : Tools and Techniques (Precedence Diagramming Method)

27. A
PMBOK Chapter 7 Project Cost Management, Section 7.4.2 Control Costs : Tools and Techniques (Variance Analysis)

Project Management Practice Questions for CAPM & PMP Exams

28. B
PMBOK Chapter 7 Project Cost Management, Section 7.4.2
Control Costs : Tools and Techniques (Variance Analysis)

Schedule Variance (SV) = EV - PV

$PV = \$500 + \$900 + \$800 = \$2,200$
$EV = \$500 + \$900 + (\$800*.75) = \$2,000$
$SV = 2,000 - 2,200 = (-200)$

A negative Schedule Variance indicates the status as behind schedule.

29. D
PMBOK Chapter 7 Project Cost Management, Section 7.4.2
Control Costs : Tools and Techniques (Variance Analysis)

Cost Performance Index (CPI) = EV / AC

$EV = \$500 + \$900 + (\$800*.75) = \$2,000$
$AC = \$2,500$
$CPI = 2000 / 2500 = 0.80$

A Cost Performance Index less than zero determines the status to be over budget.

30. C
PMBOK Chapter 7 Project Cost Management, Section 7.4.2
Control Costs : Tools and Techniques (Forecasting)

Estimate at Completion (EAC) = AC + ETC

Estimate to Completion (ETC) = BAC - EV

$BAC = \$10,000$
$EV = \$500 + \$900 + (\$800*.75) = \$2,000$
$AC = \$2,500$
$ETC = \$10,000 - \$2,000 = \$8,000$
$EAC = \$2,500 + \$8,000 = \$10,500$

31. B
PMBOK Chapter 7 Project Cost Management, Section 7.4.2
Control Costs : Tools and Techniques (Variance Analysis)

32. B
PMBOK Chapter 7 Project Cost Management, Section 7.4.2
Control Costs : Tools and Techniques (Forecasting)

33. D
PMBOK Chapter 8 Project Quality Management, Section 8.1 Plan Quality Management (fig 8.5 Cost of Quality)

34. B
PMBOK Chapter 8 Project Quality Management, Section 8.1 Plan Quality Management (fig 8.5 Cost of Quality)

35. D
PMBOK Chapter 8 Project Quality Management, Section 8.2 Manage Quality
PMBOK Chapter 8 Project Quality Management, Section 8.3 Control Quality

36. A
PMBOK Chapter 8 Project Quality Management, Section 8.2.2 Manage Quality : Tools and Techniques (Data Representation / Cause-and-Effect Diagrams)

37. A
PMBOK Chapter 8 Project Quality Management, Section 8.3.1 Control Quality : Inputs

38. C
PMBOK Chapter 8 Project Quality Management, Key Concepts for Project Quality Management

39. A
PMBOK Chapter 10 Project Communications Management
  Communications Channels = n (n - 1) / 2,
    where n= # of stakeholders
  *Answer A is correct since 16 * 15 / 2 = 120*

40. A, B, D, F, G
PMBOK Chapter 10 Project Communications Management, Key Concepts for Project Communication Management

41. D
PMBOK Chapter 10 Project Communications Management, Key Concepts for Project Communications Management

42. B
PMBOK Chapter 11 Project Risk Management, Section 11.5.2 Plan Risk Responses : Tools and Techniques (Strategies for Threats & Strategies for Opportunities)

43. C
PMBOK Chapter 11 Project Risk Management, Section 11.3.2 Perform Qualitative Risk Analysis : Tools and Techniques (Data Analysis / Assessment of Other Risk Parameters)

44. D
PMBOK Chapter 12 Project Procurement Management, Section 12.3.3 Control Procurements : Outputs

45. B
PMBOK Chapter 12 Project Procurement Management, Section 12.2.3 Conduct Procurements : Outputs

46. A, B, E
PMBOK Chapter 13 Project Stakeholder Management, Section 13.1.2 Identify Stakeholders : Tools and Techniques (Data Representation / Salience Model)

47.
    4
    3
    2
    5
    1

PMBOK Chapter 12 Project Procurement Management, Section 12.1.1 Plan Procurement Management : Inputs (Organizational Process Assets : Contract Types)

48. B
PMBOK Chapter 12 Project Procurement Management, Section 12.2.2 Conduct Procurements : Tools and Techniques

49. B
PMBOK Chapter 13 Project Stakeholder Management, Section 13.1.3 Identify Stakeholders : Outputs

50. A
PMBOK Part 2 The Standard for Project Management, Section 1.5 The Project Life Cycle (fig 1-3 Impact of Variables Over Time)

Practice Question Set #4 - ANSWERS

1. C

PMBOK Chapter 1 Introduction, Section 1.2 Foundational Elements

2. A

PMBOK Chapter 1 Introduction, Section 1.2 Foundational Elements

3. A, B, C

PMBOK Chapter 1 Introduction, Section 1.2.3 Relationship of Project, Program, Portfolio, and Operations Management

4. B

PMBOK Chapter 3 The Role of the Project Manager, Section 3.4 Project Manager Competences

5. A, B, D

PMBOK Chapter 2 The Environment in which Projects Operate, Section 2.4.4 Organizational Structure Types (Fig 2-1, Influences of Organizational Structures on Projects)

6. B

PMBOK Chapter 1 Introduction, Section 1.2.4.3 Phase Gate

7. A

PMBOK Chapter 1 Introduction, Section 1.2.4.1 Project and Development Life Cycles

8. B

PMBOK Chapter 4 Project Integration Management, Section 4.2.2 Develop Project Management Plan : Tools and Techniques

9. D

PMBOK Chapter 5 Project Scope Management, Section 5.6 Control Scope

10. A, C, D, E

PMBOK Chapter 4 Project Integration Management, Section 4.7 Close Project or Phase

11. A

PMBOK Chapter 5 Project Scope Management, Key Concepts for Project Scope Management

Project Management Practice Questions for CAPM & PMP Exams

12. A

PMBOK Chapter 6 Project Schedule Management, Section 6.3.2 Sequence Activities : Tools and Techniques (Precedence Diagramming Method)

13. D, E

PMBOK Chapter 6 Project Schedule Management, Section 6.5.2 Develop Schedule : Tools and Techniques (Critical Path Method)

14. C

PMBOK Chapter 6 Project Schedule Management, Section 6.5.2 Develop Schedule : Tools and Techniques (Schedule Compression)

15. A

PMBOK Chapter 7 Project Cost Management, Section 7.4.2 Control Costs : Tools and Techniques (Forecasting)

16. 4

2

3

1

PMBOK Chapter 7 Project Cost Management, Section 7.4.2 Control Costs : Tools and Techniques

$SV = EV - PV$ or, $1{,}000 - 600 = +400$,
$SV > 0$ means project is ahead of schedule (answer #4)

$CV = EV - AC$ or, $1{,}000 - 1{,}600 = -600$,
$CV < 0$ means project is over budget (answer #2)

$SV = EV - PV$ or, $1{,}000 - 1{,}600 = -600$,
$SV < 0$ means project is behind schedule (answer #3)

$CV = EV - AC$ or, $1{,}000 - 600 = +400$,
$CV > 0$ means project is under budget (answer #1)

17. C

PMBOK Chapter 7 Project Cost Management, Section 7.4.2 Control Costs : Tools and Techniques (Variance Analysis)

Cost Performance Index (CPI) = Earned Value (EV) / Actual Costs (AC), or $CPI = 75 / 50 = 1.5$

18. A, C

PMBOK Chapter 7 Project Cost Management, Section 7.4.2 Control Costs:Tools/Techniques:To-Complete Performance Index

TCPI = (BAC-EV) / (BAC-AC), or the value of the remaining work minus the remaining funds, therefore...

With a TCPI = 1.18, there is more work remaining than budgeted funds, and that a forecast would predict the project to complete over budget, unless performance levels improve.

The planned value is not a factor in calculating the TCPI and was not provided, therefore Schedule Variance cannot be determine and there is no way of telling if the project is behind or ahead of schedule.

19. A

PMBOK Chapter 8 Project Quality Management, Section 8.1.3 Plan Quality Management : Outputs

20. C

PMBOK Chapter 8 Project Quality Management, Key Concepts for Project Quality Management

21. B

PMBOK Chapter 8 Project Quality Management, Section 8.3.2 Control Quality : Tools and Techniques

22. B

PMBOK Chapter 9 Project Resource Management, Section 9.2.3 Estimate Activity Resources : Outputs

23. C

PMBOK Chapter 9 Project Resource Management, Section 9.3.3 Acquire Resources : Outputs

24. B, C, D, F

PMBOK Chapter 13 Project Stakeholder Management, Section 13.3.2 Manage Stakeholder Engagement : Tools and Techniques (Interpersonal and Team Skills)

25. C, D, F

PMBOK Chapter 9 Project Resource Management, Section 9.2.3 Estimate Activity Resources : Outputs (fig. 9.7 Sample Resource Breakdown Structure)

26. D
PMBOK Chapter 9 Project Resource Management, Section 9.5.2 Manage Team : Tools and Techniques (Conflict Management)

27. A
PMBOK Chapter 3 The Role of the Project Manager, Section 3.4.4.3 Politics, Power, and Getting Things Done

28. B
PMBOK Chapter 3 The Role of the Project Manager, Section 3.4.4.3 Politics, Power, and Getting Things Done

29. C
PMBOK Chapter 9 Project Resource Management, Trends and Emerging Practices in Project Resource Management

30. D
PMBOK Chapter 9 Project Resource Management, Section 9.4.2 Develop Team : Tools and Techniques (Training)

31. C
PMBOK Chapter 10 Project Communications Management

Communications Channels = $n(n-1)/2$, where n = # of stakeholders

Initially, Channels = $3*2/2 = 3$
Later, Channels = $7*6/2 = 21$
*$21 - 3 = 18$, therefore **Answer C** is correct*

32. D
PMBOK Chapter 10 Project Communications Management, Section 10.1 Plan Communications Management

33. D
PMBOK Chapter 4 Project Integration Management, Section 4.2.2 Develop Project Management Plan : Tools and Techniques (Meetings)

34. C
PMBOK Chapter 10 Project Communications Management, Section 10.3 Monitor Communications

Project Management Practice Questions for CAPM & PMP Exams

35. A
PMBOK Chapter 11 Project Risk Management, Key Concepts for Project Risk Management

36. B
PMBOK Chapter 11 Project Risk Management, Section 11.3.2 Perform Qualitative Risk Analysis : Tools and Techniques (Data Analysis / Risk Probability and Impact Assessment)

37. D
PMBOK Chapter 11 Project Risk Management, Section 11.3.2 Perform Qualitative Risk Analysis : Tools and Techniques

*Expected Monetary Value (EMV) = Probability * Impact*
*EVM = 5% * $12,000 = $600*

38. B
PMBOK Chapter 11 Project Risk Management, Section 11.5.2 Plan Risk Responses: Tools and Techniques (Strategies for Opportunities)

39. C
PMBOK Glossary, Section 3 Definitions

40. C
PMBOK Chapter 11 Project Risk Management, Section 11.3.2 Perform Qualitative Risk Analysis : Tools and Techniques

*Expected Monetary Value (EMV) = Probability * Impact*
*Opportunity EVM = 40% * $200,000 = + $80,000*
*Threat EVM = 20% * $40,000 = - $8,000*
$80,000 - $8,000 = $72, 000

41. A
PMBOK Chapter 12 Project Procurement Management, Section 12.1.3 Plan Procurement Management : Outputs

42. B
PMBOK Chapter 12 Project Procurement Management, Section 12.2.3 Conduct Procurements : Tools and Techniques

43. A
PMBOK Chapter 12 Project Procurement Management, Section 12.1.1.Plan Procurement Management : Inputs (Organizations Process Assets / Contract Types)

Project Management Practice Questions for CAPM & PMP Exams

44. D
PMBOK Chapter 12 Project Procurement Management, Section 12.1.1.Plan Procurement Management : Outputs (Procurement Statement of Work)

45. C
PMBOK Chapter 13 Project Stakeholder Management, Section 13.3.2.Manage Stakeholder Engagement : Tools and Techniques (Interpersonal and Team Skills)

46. B
PMBOK Chapter 13 Project Stakeholder Management, Section 13.1.2.Identify Stakeholders : Tools and Techniques (Data Representation)

47. B
PMBOK Chapter 13 Project Stakeholder Management, Section 13.2.2.Plan Stakeholder Engagement : Tools and Techniques (Data Representation / Stakeholder Engagement Assessment Matrix)

48. 3
    <u>4</u>

    <u>1</u>

    5

    <u>2</u>

PMBOK Chapter 13 Project Stakeholder Management, Section 13.2.2.Plan Stakeholder Engagement : Tools and Techniques (Data Representation / Stakeholder Engagement Assessment Matrix)

49. A
PMBOK Chapter 13 Project Stakeholder Management, Key Concepts for Project Stakeholder Management

50. A
PMBOK Part 2 The Standard for Project Management, Section 1.5 The Project Life Cycle (fig 1-3 Impact of Variables Over Time)

Project Management Practice Questions for CAPM & PMP Exams

Practice Question Set #5 - ANSWERS

1. D

PMBOK Chapter 11 Project Risk Management, Section 11.5.2 Plan Risk Responses: Tools and Techniques (Strategies for Threats)

2. B

PMBOK Chapter 8 Project Quality Management, Section 8.1 Plan Quality Management (fig 8.5 Cost of Quality)

3. A

PMBOK Chapter 10 Project Communications Management, Section 10.1.2 Plan Communications Management : Tools and Techniques (Communications Models)

4. D

PMBOK Chapter 4 Project Integration Management, Section 4.6 Perform Integrated Change Control

5. C

PMBOK Chapter 12 Project Procurement Management, Section 12.1.1 Plan Procurement Management : Inputs (Enterprise Environmental Factors)

6. C

PMBOK Chapter 11 Project Risk Management, Key Concepts for Project Risk Management

7. B

PMBOK Chapter 3 The Role of the Project Manager

8. B

PMBOK Chapter 10 Project Communications Management, Section 10.1 Plan Communications Management

9. D

PMBOK Chapter 4 Project Integration Management, Section 4.6.2 Perform Integrated Change Control : Tools and Techniques (Change Control Tools)

10. A

PMBOK Chapter 4 Project Integration Management, Section 4.3.3 Direct and Manage Project Work : Outputs (Change Requests)

11. D

PMBOK Chapter 6 Project Schedule Management, Section 6.5.2 Develop Schedule : Tools and Techniques (Critical Path Method)

The Order is placed on Monday, March 19
Delivery is scheduled for Thursday, March 22
Work Begins Friday, March 23
No Weekend Work (March 24-25)
Work Continues Monday March 26
Work Completes Tuesday, March 27

12. D

PMBOK Chapter 6 Project Schedule Management, Section 6.3.2 Sequence Activities : Tools and Techniques (Dependency Determination)

13. C

PMBOK Chapter 6 Project Schedule Management, Section 6.5.2 Develop Schedule : Tools and Techniques (Schedule Compression)

14. A

PMBOK Chapter 6 Project Schedule Management, Section 6.5.2 Develop Schedule : Tools and Techniques (Resource Optimization)

15. C

PMBOK Chapter 1 Introduction, Section 1.2 Foundational Elements

* Maintenance is not included in the project cost baseline.

16. A

PMBOK Chapter 7 Project Cost Management, Section 7.1 Plan Cost Management

17. C

PMBOK Chapter 7 Project Cost Management, Section 7.4.2 Control Costs : Tools and Techniques (Variance Analysis)

Earned Value (EV) = the sum value of activities completed
Actual Cost (AC) to actual costs incurred
Cost Variance (CV) = EV - AC
EV = $2,000 * 3/4 = $1,500
AC = $1,600
CV = 1,500 - 1,600 = (-100)

18. A

PMBOK Chapter 7 Project Cost Management, Section 7.4.2 Control Costs : Tools and Techniques

19. C

PMBOK Chapter 7 Project Cost Management, Section 7.4.2 Control Costs : Tools and Techniques (Forecasting)

20. A.

PMBOK Chapter 5 Project Scope Management, Section 5.2.3 Collect Requirements : Outputs (Requirements Documentation)

21. C

PMBOK Chapter 5 Project Scope Management, Section 5.3 Define Scope

22. D

PMBOK Chapter 8 Project Quality Management, Section 8.3.2 Control Quality : Tools and Techniques (Data Representation / Scatter Diagrams)

23. B

PMBOK Chapter 1 Introduction, Section 1.2 Foundational Elements (Table 1-1 Examples of Factors that Lead to the Creation of a Project)

24. C

PMBOK Chapter 3 The Role of the Project Manager, Section 3.4 Project Manager Competences

25. C

PMBOK Chapter 9 Project Resource Management, Section 9.5.2 Manage Team : Tools and Techniques (Interpersonal and Team Skills / Conflict Management)

26. D

PMBOK Chapter 9 Project Resource Management, Section 9.1.2 Plan Resource Management : Tools and Techniques (Assignment Matrix)

27. A

PMBOK Chapter 10 Project Communications Management, Key Concepts for Project Communications Management

28. C

PMBOK Chapter 8 Project Quality Management, Section 8.3.2 Control Quality: Tools & Techniques (Data Representation/ Control Charts)

29. D

PMBOK Chapter 11 Project Risk Management, Section 11.4.2 Perform Quantitative Risk Analysis : Tools and Techniques (Decision Tree Analysis)

    75% * 90% * 95% = 64.125%

30. A

PMBOK Chapter 6 Project Schedule Management, Section 6.5.2 Develop Schedule :Tools and Techniques (Schedule Compression)

31. D

PMBOK Part 2 The Standard for Project Management, Section 1.5 The Project Life Cycle (fig 1-3 Impact of Variables Over Time)

32. C

PMBOK Chapter 7 Project Cost Management, Section 7.3.3 Determine Budget : Outputs (Cost Baseline)

PMBOK Chapter 11 Project Risk Management, Section 11.1 Plan Risk Management

33. C

PMBOK Chapter 9 Project Resource Management, Trends and Emerging Practices in Project Resource Management (Virtual Teams/Distributed Teams)

34. C

PMBOK Chapter 7 Project Cost Management, Section 7.3.3 Determine Budget : Outputs (Cost Baseline)

PMBOK Chapter 7 Project Cost Management, Section 7.4.2 Control Costs : Tools and Techniques (Forecasting)

35. C

PMI Code of Ethics and Professional Conduct

36. B

PMBOK Chapter 6 Project Schedule Management, Section 6.6.3 Control Schedule : Outputs (Project Documents Updates / Lessons Learned Register)

37. A

PMBOK Chapter 8 Project Quality Management, Section 8.2.2 Manage Quality : Tools and Techniques

38. C

PMBOK Chapter 10 Project Communications Management, Section 10.3 Monitor Communications

39. B

PMBOK Chapter 2 The Environment in which Projects Operate, Section 2.2 Enterprise Environmental Factors

40. A

PMBOK Chapter 3 The Role of the Project Manager, Section 3.4.4.3 Politics, Power, and Getting Things Done

41. D

PMBOK Chapter 5 Project Scope Management, Key Concepts for Project Scope Management

42. C

PMBOK Chapter 12 Project Procurement Management, Section 12.1.2 Plan Procurement Management : Tools and Techniques (Make-or-Buy Analysis)

43. C

PMBOK Chapter 9 Project Resource Management, Section 9.5.2 Manage Team : Tools and Techniques (Interpersonal and Team Skills / Conflict Management)

44. D

PMBOK Chapter 1 Introduction, Section 1.2.6 Project Management Business Documents

45. B

PMBOK Chapter 5 Project Scope Management, Section 5.2.3 Collect Requirements: Outputs (Requirements Traceability Matrix)

46. B

PMBOK Chapter 6 Project Schedule Management, Section 6.5.2 Develop Schedule : Tools and Techniques (Schedule Compression)

* since Activity-X is on the critical path, crashing will allow the project to complete earlier. However, now Activity-Y has become critical path, and Activity-X will have 1 day float.

Project Management Practice Questions for CAPM & PMP Exams

47. B

PMBOK Chapter 4 Project Integration Management, Section 4.6 Perform Integrated Change Control

48. B

PMBOK Chapter 6 Project Schedule Management, Section 6.4.2 Estimate Activity Durations : Tools and Techniques

3-Point Beta = Optimistic + 4(Most Likely) + Pessimistic / 6

= (12 + 48 = 24) / 6 = 14

49. C

PMBOK Chapter 12 Project Procurement Management, Section 12.1.3 Plan Procurement Management : Tools and Techniques (Bid Documents)

PMI Code of Ethics and Professional Conduct

50. B

PMBOK Chapter 1 Introduction, Section 1.2.4.1 Project and Development Life Cycles

Practice Question Set #6 - ANSWERS

1. D

PMBOK Chapter 4 Project Integration Management, Section 4.6 Perform Integrated Change Control

2. A

PMBOK Chapter 6 Project Schedule Management, Section 6.4.2 Estimate Activity Durations : Tools and Techniques

3. C

PMBOK Chapter 5 Project Scope Management, Section 5.3.3 Define Scope : Outputs (Project Scope Statement)

4. C

PMBOK Chapter 6 Project Schedule Management, Section 6.2 Define Activities

5. C

PMBOK Chapter 1 Introduction, Section 1.2 Foundational Elements

6. B

PMBOK Chapter 12 Project Procurement Management, Section 12.1.1 Plan Procurement Management : Inputs (Organizational Process Assets / Contract Types)

7. C

PMI Code of Ethics and Professional Conduct

8. B

PMBOK Chapter 7 Project Cost Management, Section 7.4.2 Control Costs : Tools and Techniques (To-Complete Performance Index)

9. D

PMBOK Chapter 6 Project Schedule Management, Section 6.3.2 Sequence Activities : Tools & Techniques (Dependency Determination and Integration/Discretionary Dependencies)

10. C

PMBOK Chapter 6 Project Schedule Management, Section 6.4.2 Estimate Activity Durations : Tools and Techniques

* *3-point Beta = [Optimistic + 4(Most Likely) + Pessimistic] / 6*

[3 + (4*12) + 15] / 6 = 11

11. B

PMBOK Chapter 1 Introduction, Section 1.2.4.1 Project and Development Life Cycles

PMBOK Chapter 5 Project Scope Management, Section 5.4.2.Create WBS : Tools and Techniques (Decomposition)

12. B

PMBOK Chapter 6 Project Schedule Management, Section 6.3.2 Sequence Activities : Tools and Techniques (Dependency Determination and Integration)

13. B

PMBOK Chapter 13 Project Schedule Management, Section 13.3.2 Manage Stakeholder Engagement : Tools and Techniques (Expert Judgement, Communications Skills)

PMBOK Chapter 3 The Role of the Project Manager, Section 3.4 Project Manager Competences (Leadership)

PMI Code of Ethics and Professional Conduct

14. A

PMBOK Chapter 6 Project Schedule Management, Section 6.5.2 Develop Schedule : Tools and Techniques (Critical Path Method)

15. A

PMBOK Chapter 7 Project Schedule Management, Section 7.3.2 Determine Budget : Tools and Techniques (Data Analysis)

16. C

PMBOK Chapter 11 Project Risk Management, Key Concepts for Project Risk Management

17. B

PMBOK Chapter 1 Introduction, Section 1.2.4.1 Project and Development Life Cycles

18. C

PMBOK Chapter 7 Project Cost Management, Section 7.4.2 Control Costs : Tools and Techniques (Variance Analysis/Schedule Performance Index)

19. B

PMBOK Chapter 7 Project Cost Management, Section 7.4.2 Control Costs : Tools and Techniques (Variance Analysis)

20. B
PMBOK Chapter 4 Project Integration Management, Section 4.6 Perform Integrated Change Control

21. A
PMBOK Glossary, Section 3 Definitions

22. C
PMBOK Chapter 8 Project Quality Management, Section 8.1 Plan Quality Management (fig 8.5 Cost of Quality)

23. A
PMBOK Chapter 4 Project Integration Management, Section 4.2.2 Develop Project Management Plan : Tools and Techniques (Meetings)

24. C
PMBOK Chapter 7 Project Cost Management, Section 7.4.2 Control Costs : Tools and Techiques (To-Complete Performance Index)

    * TCPI = (BAC-EV) / (BAC-AC)
       (100,000-60,000) / (100,000-75,000) = 1.6

25. C
PMI Code of Ethics and Professional Conduct

26. D
PMBOK Chapter 12 Project Procurement Management, Key Concepts for Project Procurement Management

27. A
PMBOK Chapter 4 Project Integration Management, Section 4.3 Direct and Manage Project Work

28. A
PMBOK Chapter 11 Project Risk Management, Section 11.3.2 Perform Quantitative Risk Analysis : Decision Tree Analysis

    Capacity for existing/renovated theater is 1,000
    Capacity for new theater is 75% greater, or 1,750
    Investment for Build is $12 million
    Investment for Renovate is $5 million
    *Revenue = ticket price * capacity * # of performances*
    *EMV = (Revenue - Investment) * probability*

EMV for Build =
  *Strong Demand [(100 * 1,750 * 200) - 12,000,000] * .6*
+ Weak Demand [(100 875 * 200) - 12,000,000] * .4*
        = $13.8m (strong) + $2.2m (weak) = $16m
EMV for Renovation =
  *Strong Demand [(100 * 1,000 * 200) - 5,000,000] * .6*
+ Weak Demand [(100 500 * 200) - 5,000,000] * .4*
        = $9m (strong) + $2m (weak)   = $11m

Therefore, Build requires a greater investment ($12m vs. $5m), but returns a greater EMV ($16m vs $11m)

29. A
PMBOK Chapter 11 Project Risk Management, Section 11.4.2 Perform Quantitative Risk Analysis : Tools & Techniques (Data Analysis/Simulations)

30. C
PMBOK Chapter 4 Project Integration Management, Section 4.7 Close Project or Phase

31. C
PMBOK Chapter 4 Project Integration Management, Section 4.1.1 Develop Project Charter : Inputs

32. B
PMBOK Chapter 9 Project Resource Management, Section 9.2.3 Estimate Activity Resources : Outputs (Resource Breakdown)

33. C
PMBOK Chapter 8 Project Quality Management, Section 8.3.2 Control Quality : Tools and Techniques (Inspection)

34. A
PMBOK Chapter 8 Project Quality Management, Section 8.1.2 Plan Quality Management : Tools and Techniques (Cost of Quality)

35. A
PMBOK Chapter 9 Project Resource Management, Section 9.4 Develop Team

36. C
PMBOK Chapter 9 Project Resource Management, Section 9.5.2 Manage Team : Tools and Techniques (Interpersonal and Team Skills / Conflict Management)

37. B
PMBOK Chapter 5 Project Scope Management, Key Concepts for Project Scope Management

38. D
PMBOK Chapter 5 Project Scope Management, Section 5.2.2 Collect Requirements : Tools and Techniques (Data Representation / Mind Mapping)

39. D
PMBOK Chapter 6 Project Schedule Management, Section 6.3.2 Sequence Activities: Tools and Techniques (Leads and Lags)

40. A
PMBOK Chapter 13 Project Stakeholder Management, Section 13.1.2 Identify Stakeholders : Tools & Techniques (Data Representation / Salience Model)

41. B
PMBOK Chapter 6 Project Schedule Management, Section 6.5.2 Develop Schedule :Tools and Techniques (Critical Path Method)

42. C
PMBOK Chapter 5 Project Scope Management, Section 5.2.2 Collect Requirements : Tools & Techniques (Context Diagram)

43. A
PMBOK Chapter 11 Project Risk Management, Section 11.4.2 Perform Quantitative Risk Analysis : Tools and Techniques

44. B
PMBOK Chapter 11 Project Risk Management, Section 11.5.2 Plan Risk Responses : Tools and Techniques (Strategies for Threats)

45. B
PMBOK Chapter 6 Project Schedule Management, Section 6.5.2 Develop Schedule : Tools & Techniques (Critical Path Method)

    Early Finish Date = Week-10
    Late Finish Date = Week-13
    13 - 10 = 3 weeks

46. D
PMBOK Chapter 6 Project Schedule Management, Section 6.5.2 Develop Schedule : Tools and Techniques (Resource Optimization / Resource Leveling)

47. C
PMBOK Chapter 5 Project Scope Management, Section 5.5.1 Validate Scope : Inputs

48. A
PMBOK Chapter 12 Project Procurement Management, Section 12.1.3 Plan Procurement Management: Outputs (Procurement Strategy)

49. C
PMBOK Chapter 8 Project Quality Management, Section 8.2.2 Manage Quality : Tools & Techniques (Data Representation/Scatter Diagram)

50. C
PMBOK Chapter 10 Project Communication Management, Section 10.3 Monitor Communications

Project Management Practice Questions for CAPM & PMP Exams

Practice Question Set #7 - ANSWERS

1. A
PMBOK Chapter 10 Project Communications Management, Section 10.1.2 Plan Communications Management : Tools and Techniques (Communications Models)
PMP Examination Content Outline (For July 2020 Exams), Domain 1: People, Task 2: Lead a Team : Support Diversity and Inclusion

2. A
PMP Examination Content Outline (For July 2020 Exams), Domain 1: People, Task 2: Lead a Team : Determine the Appropriate Leadership Style

3. A
PMP Examination Content Outline (For July 2020 Exams), Domain 1: People, Task 1: Manage Conflict : Interpret the Source and Stage of Conflict
PMP Examination Content Outline (For July 2020 Exams), Domain 1: People, Task 10: Build Shared Understanding : Break Down the Situation to Find the Root Cause of Misunderstanding

4. B
PMBOK Chapter 10 Project Communication Management, Key Concepts for Project Communication Management

5. C
PMBOK Chapter 9 Project Resource Management, Section 9.5.2 Manage Team : Tools and Techniques (Interpersonal and Team Skills / Conflict Management)
PMP Examination Content Outline (For July 2020 Exams), Domain 1: People, Task 9: Collaborate With Stakeholders : Build Trust & Influence Stakeholders to Accomplish Project Objectives

6. B
PMBOK Chapter 9 Project Resource Management, Trends and Emerging Practices in Project Resource Management
PMP Examination Content Outline (For July 2020 Exams), Domain 1: People, Task 14: Promote Team Performance through the Application of Emotional Intelligence

7. B
PMBOK Chapter 3 The Role of the Project Manager, 3.4.5 Leadership Styles

PMP Examination Content Outline (For July 2020 Exams), Domain 1: People, Task 2: Lead a Team : Inspire, Motivate, and Influence Team Members/Stakeholders

PMP Examination Content Outline (For July 2020 Exams), Domain 1: People, Task 3: Support Team Performance : Support and Recognize Team Member Growth and Development

8. D

PMBOK Chapter 9 Project Resource Management, Section 9.4 Develop Team

PMP Examination Content Outline (For July 2020 Exams), Domain 1: People, Task 11: Engage and Support Virtual Teams

9. D

PMBOK Chapter 9 Project Resource Management, Section 9.4.2 Develop Team : Tools and Techniques (Recognition and Rewards)

PMP Examination Content Outline (For July 2020 Exams), Domain 1: People, Task 3: Support Team Performance : Determine Appropriate Feedback Approach

10. D

PMBOK Chapter 4 Project Integration Management, Section 4.4 Manage Project Knowledge

11. C

PMP Examination Content Outline (For July 2020 Exams), Domain 1: People, Task 2: Lead a Team: Servant Leadership

12. B

PMBOK Chapter 9 Project Resource Management, Section 9.5.2 Manage Team : Tools and Techniques (Interpersonal and Team Skills / Conflict Management)

PMP Examination Content Outline (For July 2020 Exams), Domain 1: People, Task 1: Manage Conflict : Evaluate, Recommend, Reconcile the Appropriate Conflict Resolution Solution

13. C

PMBOK Chapter 9 Project Resource Management, Section 9.5.2 Manage Team : Tools & Techniques: Interpersonal & Team Skills

PMP Examination Content Outline (For July 2020 Exams), Domain 1: People, Task 14: Promote Team Performance through the Application of Emotional Intelligence

PMP Examination Content Outline (For July 2020 Exams), Domain 1: People, Task 4: Empower Team and Stakeholders

14. C
PMBOK Chapter 13 Project Stakeholder Management, Section 13.1.2 Identify Stakeholders : Tools & Techniques (Data Representation / Salience Model)

PMP Examination Content Outline (For July 2020 Exams), Domain 1: People, Task 9: Collaborate with Stakeholders : Optimize Alignment between Stakeholder Needs, Expectations, and Project Objectives

15. A
PMBOK Chapter 9 Project Resource Management, Trends and Emerging Practices in Project Resource Management : Tailoring Considerations

PMBOK Chapter 10 Project Communication Management, Key Concepts for Project Communication Management (Cultural Awareness)

PMBOK Chapter 13 Project Stakeholder Management, Trends and Emerging Practices in Project Resource Management : Tailoring Considerations

PMP Examination Content Outline (For July 2020 Exams), Domain 1: People, Task 2: Lead a Team : Support Diversity and Inclusion, and Task 10: Build a Shared Understanding

16. A
PMBOK Chapter 9 Project Resource Management, Section 9.5.2 Manage Team : Tools & Techniques (Interpersonal and Team Skills/Conflict Management)

PMP Examination Content Outline (For July 2020 Exams), Domain 1: People, Task 1: Manage Conflict : Analyze the Context of the Conflict

17. B
PMP Examination Content Outline (For July 2020 Exams), Domain 1: People, Task 2: Lead a Team : Determine the Appropriate Leadership Style

18. A
PMBOK Chapter 4 Project Integration Management, Section 4.7 Close Project or Phase

19. D
PMBOK Chapter 13 Project Stakeholder Management, Section 13.3.2 Manage Stakeholder Engagement : Tools and Techniques (Interpersonal and Team Skills)

20. D
PMP Examination Content Outline (For July 2020 Exams), Domain 1: People, Task 14: Promote Team Performance through the Application of Emotional Intelligence

21. A
PMBOK Chapter 10 Project Communication Management, Key Concepts for Project Communication Management

22. D
PMBOK Chapter 3 The Role of the Project Manager, Section 3.4 Project Manager Competencies (Personality Indicators)

PMP Examination Content Outline (For July 2020 Exams), Domain 1: People, Task 14: Promote Team Performance through the Application of Emotional Intelligence (Assess Behavior through the Use of Personality Indicators)

23. A
PMP Examination Content Outline (For July 2020 Exams), Domain 1: People, Task 7: Address and Remove Impediments, Obstacles, and Blockers for the Team

PMP Examination Content Outline (For July 2020 Exams), Domain 1: People, Task 2: Lead a Team : Value Servant Leadership

24. A
PMBOK Chapter 13 Project Stakeholder Management, Section 13.1.2 Plan Stakeholder Engagement : Tools & Techniques (Data Representation/Power-Interest Grid)

PMP Examination Content Outline (For July 2020 Exams), Domain 1: People, Task 9: Collaborate with Stakeholders : Evaluate Engagement Needs for Stakeholders

25. B
PMP Examination Content Outline (For July 2020 Exams), Domain 1: People, Task 2: Lead a Team : Determine the Appropriate Leadership Style

26. C
PMBOK Chapter 3 The Role of the Project Manager, Section 3.4.4.3 Politics, Power, and Getting Things Done

PMP Examination Content Outline (For July 2020 Exams), Domain 1: People, Task 2: Lead a Team : Analyze Team Member and Stakeholder Influence

27. B

PMBOK Chapter 4 Project Integration Management, Section 4.4. Manage Project Knowledge

PMP Examination Content Outline (For July 2020 Exams), Domain 1: People, Task 9: Collaborate with Stakeholders: Build Trust and Influence Stakeholders to Accomplish Project Objectives

28. D

PMBOK Chapter 9 Project Resource Management, Section 9.4.2 Develop Team : Tools and Techniques (Training)

PMP Examination Content Outline (For July 2020 Exams), Domain 1: People, Task 5: Ensure Team Members and Stakeholders are Adequately Trained

29. B

PMBOK Chapter 9 Project Resource Management, Section 9.2.2 Manage Team : Tools & Techniques (Interpersonal and Team Skills/Emotional Intelligence)

PMP Examination Content Outline (For July 2020 Exams), Domain 1: People, Task 14: Promote Team Performance through the Application of Emotional Intelligence (Assess Behavior through the Use of Personality Indicators)

30. A

PMBOK Chapter 3 The Role of the Project Manager, 3.4.5 Management vs Leadership (Personality)

31. C

PMBOK Chapter 9 Project Resource Management, Section 9.5.3 Manage Team : Tools & Techniques (Interpersonal and Team Skills/Influencing)

32. B

PMBOK Chapter 10 Project Communications Management, Section 10.1.2 Plan Communications Management : Tools & Techniques (Communications Methods)

33. C

PMBOK Chapter 13 Project Stakeholder Management, Section 13.3.2.Manage Stakeholder Engagement : Tools and Techniques (Interpersonal and Team Skills)

PMP Examination Content Outline (For July 2020 Exams), Domain 1: People, Task 13: Mentor Relevant Stakeholders (Recognize and Act on Opportunities)

Project Management Practice Questions for CAPM & PMP Exams

34. C
PMI Code of Ethics and Professional Conduct

35. A
PMBOK Chapter 11 Project Risk Management, 11.7.2 Monitor Risks : Tools and Techniques (Risk Audit)

36. D
PMBOK Chapter 13 Project Stakeholder Management, Section 13.3 Manage Stakeholder Engagement

PMP Examination Content Outline (For July 2020 Exams), Domain 1: People, Task 9: Collaborate with Stakeholders (Build Trust and Influence Stakeholders to Accomplish Project Objectives)

37. A
PMBOK Chapter 13 Project Stakeholder Management, Section 13.2.2.Plan Stakeholder Engagement : Tools and Techniques (Stakeholder Engagement Assessment Matrix)

PMP Examination Content Outline (For July 2020 Exams), Domain 1: People, Task 9: Collaborate with Stakeholders (Optimize Alignment Between Stakeholder Needs, Expectations, and Project Objectives)

38. A
PMBOK Chapter 9 Project Resource Management, Section 9.5.3 Manage Team : Tools & Techniques (Interpersonal and Team Skills/Cultural Awareness)

PMP Examination Content Outline (For July 2020 Exams), Domain 1: People, Task 2: Lead a Team : Support Diversity and Inclusion

39. C
PMBOK Chapter 10 Project Communication Management, Section 10.2.2 Manage Commnications : Tools & Techniques (Meeting Management)

40. B
PMBOK Chapter 3 The Role of the Project Manager, 3.4.5 Management vs Leadership (Personality)

PMBOK Chapter 11 Project Risk Management, 3.5 Plan Risk Response

PMP Examination Content Outline (For July 2020 Exams), Domain 1: People, Task 4: Empower Team and Stakeholders (Organize Around Team Strengths)

41. A

PMBOK Chapter 9 Project Resource Management, Section 9.5.2 Manage Team : Tools and Techniques (Interpersonal Skills/Emotional Intelligence)

PMP Examination Content Outline (For July 2020 Exams), Domain 1: People, Task 14: Promote Team Performance through the Application of Emotional Intelligence

42. D

43. B

PMBOK Chapter 13 Project Schedule Management, Section 13.3.2 Manage Stakeholder Engagement : Tools and Techniques (Expert Judgment, Communications Skills)

PMBOK Chapter 3 The Role of the Project Manager, Section 3.4 Project Manager Competences (Leadership)

PMI Code of Ethics and Professional Conduct

44. D

PMBOK Chapter 4 Project Integration Management, Section 4.2.2 Develop Project Management Plan : Tools and Techniques (Meetings)

45. B

PMBOK Chapter 13 Project Stakeholder Management, Section 13.4 Monitor Stakeholder Engagement

PMP Examination Content Outline (For July 2020 Exams), Domain 1: People, Task 9: Collaborate with Stakeholders (Optimize Alignment Between Stakeholder Needs, Expectations, and Project Objectives)

46. B

PMBOK Chapter 10 Project Communication Management, Key Concepts for Project Communication Management

47. C

PMBOK Chapter 10 Project Communication Management, Key Concepts for Project Communication Management

48. B

PMBOK Chapter 9 Project Resource Management, Section 9.3.2 Acquire Resources : Tools and Techniques (Decision Making)

PMP Examination Content Outline (For July 2020 Exams), Domain 1: People, Task 2: Lead a Team : Support Diversity and Inclusion

49. A
PMBOK Chapter 3 The Role of the Project Manager, 3.4.5 Management vs Leadership (Personality)

PMP Examination Content Outline (For July 2020 Exams), Domain 1: People, Task 2: Lead a Team : Distinguish Various Options to Lead Team Members and Stakeholders

50. D
PMBOK Chapter 11 Project Communication Management, Key Concepts for Communications Management

PMP Examination Content Outline (For July 2020 Exams), Domain 1: People, Task 8: Negotiate Project Agreements : Verify Objectives of the Project Agreement are Met

Practice Question Set #8 - ANSWERS

1. B
Agile Practice Guide, Section 2.4 Uncertainty, Risk, and Life Cycle Selection
PMBOK Chapter 11 Project Risk Management, Considerations for Agile/Adaptive Environments

2. B
Agile Practice Guide Sections 4.3.1 Agile Teams (table 4-2 Agile Team Roles)

3. D
Agile Practice Guide, Section 5.4 Measurements in Agile Projects
PMBOK Chapter 11 Project Risk Management, Section 11.4.2 Perform Quantitative Risk Analysis (Tools & Techniques)

4. D
Agile Practice Guide, Section 5.2.4 Daily Standups
PMBOK Chapter 10 Project Communication Management, Trends and Emerging Practices in Project Communication Management

5. A
Agile Practice Guide, Section 5.2.1 Retrospectives
PMBOK Chapter 8 Project Quality Management, Section 8.3.2 Control Quality (Tools & Techniques/Meetings)

6. A
Agile Practice Guide, Section 4.2 Servant Leadership Empowers the Team

7. C
Agile Practice Guide, Section 5.4 Measurements in Agile Projects
PMBOK Chapter 6 Project Schedule Management, Section 6.6.2 Control Schedule : Tools and Techniques (Iteration Burndown Chart)

8. B
Agile Practice Guide, Section 2.2 The Agile Manifesto and Mindset (fig 2-2 The 12 Principles Behind the Agile Manifesto

9. A
Agile Practice Guide, Section 3.1.3 Characteristics of Incremental Life Cycles

Project Management Practice Questions for CAPM & PMP Exams

Agile Practice Guide, Section 5.4 Measurements in Agile Projects

PMBOK Chapter 6 Project Schedule Management, Section 6.6.2 Control Schedule : Tools and Techniques (Iteration Burndown Chart)

10. B

Agile Practice Guide, Section 3.1.5 Agile Suitability Filters

PMBOK Chapter 1 Introduction, Section 1.2.4.1 Project and Development Life Cycles

11. C

Agile Practice Guide, Section 2.4 Uncertainty, Risk, and Life Cycle Selection

12. C

Agile Practice Guide, Section 3.1.3 Characteristics of Incremental Life Cycles

PMBOK Chapter 6 Project Schedule Management, Considerations for Agile/Adaptive Environments

13. A

Agile Practice Guide, Section 3.1.5 Agile Suitability Filters

PMBOK Chapter 1 Introduction, Section 1.2.4.1 Project and Development Life Cycles

14. C

Agile Practice Guide, Section 3.1.5 Agile Suitability Filters

PMBOK Chapter 1 Introduction, Section 1.2.4.1 Project and Development Life Cycles

15. D

Agile Practice Guide, Section 5.4.1 Agile Teams Measure Results (fig 5.3 Kanban Board)

16. A

Agile Practice Guide, Section 5.4 Measurements in Agile Projects (fig 5.2 Burnup Chart)

PMBOK Chapter 6 Project Schedule Management, Section 6.6.2 Control Schedule : Tools & Techniques (Iteration Burndown Chart)

17. C

Agile Practice Guide, Section 5.2.2 Backlog Preparation and 5.2.3 Backlog Refinement

18. B
Agile Practice Guide, Section 6.2.1 Creating an Environment of Safety

PMBOK Chapter 10 Project Communications Management, Considerations for Agile/Adaptive Environments

19. A
Agile Practice Guide, Section 5.4 Measurements in Agile Projects (fig 5.1 Burndown Chart)

PMBOK Chapter 6 Project Schedule Management, Section 6.6.2 Control Schedule : Tools & Techniques (Iteration Burndown Chart)

20. B
Agile Practice Guide, Section 6.5 Multi-Team Coordination and Dependencies (Scaling)

Agile Practice Guide, Annex A3.10 Scaling Frameworks

21. A
Agile Practice Guide, Section 4.2.1 Servant Leader Responsibilites

22. D
Agile Practice Guide, Section 5.2.1 Retrospectives

PMBOK Chapter 8 Project Quality Management, Section 8.3.2 Control Quality (Tools & Techniques/Meetings)

23. C
Agile Practice Guide, Section 2.3 Lean and Kanban Method, plus Annex A3-2 Scrum and A3-4 Kanban

24. A
PMBOK Chapter 10 Project Communications Management, Considerations for Agile/Adaptive Environments

25. B
Agile Practice Guide, Section 3.1.5 Agile Suitability Filters

PMBOK Chapter 1 Introduction, Section 1.2.4.1 Project and Development Life Cycles

26. C
Agile Practice Guide, Section 5.2.2 Backlog Preparation and 5.2.3 Backlog Refinement

PMBOK Chapter 5 Project Scope Management, Key Concepts for Project Scope Management & Considerations for Agile/Adaptive Environments

Project Management Practice Questions for CAPM & PMP Exams

PMBOK Chapter 6 Project Schedule Management, Section 6.4.2 Estimate Activity Durations : Tools and Techniques (Meetings)

27. D
Agile Practice Guide, Section 5.2.5 Demonstrations/Reviews

28. D
Agile Practice Guide, Section 5.2.6 Planning for Iteration-based Agile

29. A
Agile Practice Guide, Section 5.2.3 Backlog Refinement
PMBOK Chapter 5 Project Scope Management, Key Concepts for Project Scope Management & Considerations for Agile/Adaptive Environments

30. A
Agile Practice Guide, Section 5.4 Measurements in Agile Projects
Agile Practice Guide, Section 5.6 Planning for Iteration-based Agile

31. A
Agile Practice Guide, Glossary (Terms and Definitions)

32. C
Agile Practice Guide, Section 5.4 Measurements in Agile Projects

33. D
Agile Practice Guide, Section 5.2.2 Backlog Preparation and 5.2.3 Backlog Refinement

34. B
Agile Practice Guide, Section 2.3 Lean and the Kanban Method

35. C
Agile Practice Guide, Section 5.2.6 Planning for Iteration-based Agile

36. C
Agile Practice Guide, Section 6.1.1 Drivers for Change Management

37. A
Agile Practice Guide, Section 2.3 Lean and Kanban Method, and Glossary

38. A
Agile Practice Guide, Section 5.2.7 Execution Practices That Help Teams Deliver Value

39. B
Agile Practice Guide, Annex A3.3 Extreme Programming (XP)

40. B
Agile Practice Guide, Section 5.2.1 Retrospectives

41. C
Agile Practice Guide, Section 4.3.5 Dedicated Teams

42. C
Agile Practice Guide, Section 5.2.5 Demonstrations/Review

43. A
Agile Practice Guide, Section 4.2.1 Servant Leader Responsibilities

44. D
Agile Practice Guide, Section 5.2.2 Backlog Preparation and 5.2.3 Backlog Refinement

45. D
Agile Practice Guide, Section 2.2 The Agile Manifesto & Mindset

46. C
Agile Practice Guide, Section 4.2.1 Servant Leader Responsibilites

47. B
Agile Practice Guide, Section 5.2.2 Backlog Preparation and 5.2.3 Backlog Refinement

PMBOK Chapter 5 Project Scope Management, Key Concepts for Project Scope Management & Considerations for Agile/Adaptive Environments

48. B
Agile Practice Guide

Agile Practice Guide, Section 3.1.5 Agile Suitability Filters

PMBOK Chapter 1 Introduction, Section 1.2.4.1 Project and Development Life Cycles

49. D
Agile Practice Guide, Glossary

50. B
Agile Practice Guide, Section 5.2.2 Backlog Preparation and 5.2.3 Backlog Refinement

PMBOK Chapter 5 Project Scope Management, Key Concepts for Project Scope Management & Considerations for Agile/Adaptive Environments

Notes

Made in the USA
Las Vegas, NV
26 January 2021